GYM PSYCH

THE INSIDER'S GUIDE TO HEALTH CLUBS

THE INSIDER'S GUIDE TO HEALTH CLUBS

Maury Z. Levy
and
Jay Shafran

Fawcett Columbine New York

For Sue forever—M.Z.L.
For Mom and Dad—J.S.

A Fawcett Columbine Book
Published by Ballantine Books
Copyright © 1986 by Maury Z. Levy and Jay Shafran

All rights reserved under International and Pan-American Copyright Conventions. Published in the United States by Ballantine Books, a division of Random House, Inc., New York, and simultaneously in Canada by Random House of Canada Limited, Toronto.

Library of Congress Catalog Card Number: 85-90898

ISBN: 0-449-90171-8

Cover design by Barry Littman
Book design by Beth Tondreau
Manufactured in the United States of America

First Edition: August 1986
10 9 8 7 6 5 4 3 2 1

CONTENTS

GYM PSYCH—AN INTRODUCTION	1
YOU CAN'T START A FIRE WITHOUT A SPARK	9
A TYPING TEST	23
PSYCHING UP	35
JOIN THE CLUB	45
HOW TO CHOOSE A TRAINER	69
HOW TO WORK OUT	79
THE GYM PSYCH EXERCISE GUIDE	93

THE GYM PSYCH FASHION GUIDE	101
THE SEX CHAPTER	113
HURTS SO GOOD	123
SWEATING WITH THE STARS	133
EXPLODING THE MYTHS	143

ACKNOWLEDGMENTS

We'd like to exercise our right to thank the following people for their help and support. We couldn't have done this book without them. Well, let's not get carried away. We couldn't have done this book without our parents. Basic biology. But these folks did make life a lot easier:

Paul Levy, who is one great editor; Daniel Levy, who is one great friend; and Scott Levy, who is still the fastest white boy in New Jersey. Mona Plumer, who worked well above and way beyond the call. Jan Harayda, Andi Sporkin, Jim Petersen, and Dorothy Cupich, for helping cover the country. Lise Spiegel, Linda Wells, Mike

Motta, Chris Meade, and Christine Haycock for valuable research. Hollis Wayne for fashion guidance. Michelle Russell, Nancy Novogrod, and Amanda Urban for motivation. Yogi Berra and Thomas Jefferson for inspiration. Maddie for Wednesdays. And Elaine Powers, our close personal friend, for the pepperoni.

GYM PSYCH— AN INTRODUCTION

It's about Cher. You know Cher. She's the skinny woman who used to sing with the short guy. So now here's Cher appearing in these national ads for health clubs. You know the ads. You pay something like forty-nine bucks for the rest of your life and they let you into these places, and with any luck at all, you come out looking like Cher. You do want to look like Cher, don't you? No? Well, then how about you women?

Of course, Cher is just the latest role model for the fitness revolution. She was preceded by Victoria Principal, Eláine Powers, Jack LaLanne, Charles Atlas, and

2 GYM PSYCH

Plato, who was really the founder of fitness as well as relationships between people who aren't turned on by each other.

The first gyms (they were still called gymnasiums back then) appeared in Greece in about, oh, the fourth century B.C. They were so large and elaborate that they had to be built on the outskirts of town, in the suburbs, out near the shopping mall with the Häagen-Dazs store.

The first gyms boasted well-watered groves, trim walks and avenues, riding schools, plenty of masseurs and instructors, but not a whole lot of Nautilus machines. It was at these gyms that Plato went one-on-one with Aristotle. They would gather their students and followers around them and give long dissertations about the deeper meanings of life. This was before juice bars.

It was thought then that a healthy body and a fertile mind went together. Several years later, Jack LaLanne would say this on his televison show. It took a while to catch on. But then so did Jack LaLanne. Fifty years ago, when he opened his first gym in Oakland, he had to beg people to come in and work out. Eventually, the idea attracted enough men. And women, then a weaker sex, soon found their own form of exercise. Usually, that meant standing in front of a machine with a belt around your butt and jiggling like Jell-O.

From there, fitness caught on like jock itch. Jack Kennedy took a long walk and the country went along. Then people started playing tennis and John McEnroe came out of nowhere and Billie Jean King came out of the closet. Next came jogging and shin splints and running and racquetball and Nikes that glowed in the dark.

Finally, America was off its ass. Men lost their beer bellies, women their saddle bags, and there was nothing left to do but firm up what was left. That's where health clubs came in.

AN INTERVIEW WITH ELAINE POWERS

"Hello, Elaine Powers."
"Hi, is this her? Is this Elaine?"
"No."
"Well, is she there?"
"No, see there really ain't no Elaine Powers."
"What?"
"No, they just named the places Elaine Powers because they thought it sounded good. You know, to be named after a real person instead of a company. Like they thought women would really identify with that."
"Who are 'they'?"
"Oh, the men who own it."

At first, health clubs had a lot in common with Orthodox Judaism. The men would always be separate from the women. Different rooms, different routines, different machines. But soon, and this is why you don't see many Orthodox synagogues any more, the sexes started mingling. They met around the pool, the jacuzzi, the lounge. They traded phone numbers and they traded notes. They realized that women weren't as weak as some people thought they were, that women could really work on machines, just like men. And that men could start doing some of the women's stuff, too. Like aerobics and calisthenics. Just as long as no one called it Slimnastics or "tummy tightening." While women had lost their inhibitions, men hadn't yet lost their minds.

And so, the current-day clubs came to pass. Gleaming torture chambers where people in purple leotards could be at one with iron horses. Places where grown men came to prove they were grown men. Places where women ran through the *Kama Sutra* on aerobic mats. Investment bankers and housewives, fashion models and computer programmers; the multitudes came flocking to these new temples of workout.

While some spots remained spartan, the most popular had gone glittery. (Disco had to go somewhere.) The glitzy gyms had the greatest growth. Full-service coed facilities started to pop up like triceps. Fitness became a business, then an industry. Today, over seventy-five million people are exercising, spending close to $30 billion on fitness. That's billion with a "b."

Great news? Yes and no. It's true that the fitness boom is affecting our very lifestyle. You see it everywhere—less red meat sold, more money spent on eyeliners that don't run when you sweat. But it's not a total success. Not yet. Too many people are wasting their money, stuck in bad programs, discouraged by failure. The drop-out rate at many health clubs is estimated to be as high as 90 percent. Why? The fitness boom happened too fast. People started running into gyms before the folks who ran the gyms knew what to do with them.

And that's not what fitness is supposed to be about. Too many people started doing too much too fast, with little or no supervision. This didn't lead to body tone, only frustration and injury. The quick fix didn't fix anyone. It's only recently that fitness fanatics started to realize that there was no such thing as instant results, no matter what Jane Fonda said. True fitness is a lifestyle. It should be taught by experts, not movie stars. It's a very personal thing that needs to be organized, supervised, and individualized. Even if we are all wearing the same aerobic shoes.

If fitness is going to work, it's going to have to be well-rounded. And that'll happen. Exercise studios will be replaced by total fitness centers where fruit drinks won't be the only thing mixed. Diet will be mixed with technology. Exercise will be mixed with motivation. As Plato would have wanted, we'll finally combine the body with the mind. Physiology with psychology. Gym with psych.

And that's what this book is about. Oh, we know you've sneaked a peek at other books. You know the ones. There are two kinds on the market now. There are the celebrity books: Jane and John and Christie show you some pretty pictures and offer you a bit of help and a lot of glitz. Then there are the buff books—the technical tomes that offer a lot of guts as well as complete instruction on how to take a Nautilus machine apart in your spare time.

What no one has really done is to write a book that bridges the gap. Until now. *Gym Psych* is guts and glitz with style. It holds up the ultimate mirror to the gym generation, the people who have all the right sneakers but none of the right answers.

Gym Psych is for the gym rat—the person who's already

hooked but needs to know more. Stick with us and you'll learn how to sag your socks. And *Gym Psych* is for the person who's already joined a health club but feels intimidated by it. We'll show you that a bench press doesn't mean ironing your pants in the park. But, most of all, *Gym Psych* is for those of you who have almost no idea how to restore order to your pects; those of you who've been sitting on the sidelines while everyone else puts a down payment on those neon wristbands and gets a second lease on life; those of you who've wanted to get more involved but just didn't know where to start.

We'll give you just the edge you need—the critical psychological edge over the system itself. We won't try to sell you on a particular machine or routine. We won't even try to sell you a videotape. Simply, the purpose of *Gym Psych* is to put the whole fitness boom into perspective for you—to demystify the process and make the gym more accessible. And to teach you not to take certain things too seriously. Life, for those of you keeping score at home, is too short. We hope you'll come away from this book realizing that putting your tongue in your cheek is just as important an exercise as touching your fingers to your toes.

There's much more to fitness than sweat. *Gym Psych* is gym chic. It's how to be cool around the gym. It's how to choose a gym by how it's outfitted and how to outfit yourself for the gym you choose. It's setting your fitness goals and reaching them; learning how to stick with it; knowing how to connect your knee bone to your thigh bone and your muscles to your brain. It's learning how to play mind games and knowing how to keep it simple. It's figuring what type you are and how to live within yourself. It's knowing what counts and how to score at the gym. It's getting psyched like the pros and finding out how to deal with fear, guilt, intimidation, and women who wear strange underwear. It's knowing when to lay back and when to stand up for what's yours. It's how to psych up and how to work out. It's reading about the fifty top clubs in America and finding the right one in your neighborhood. It's learning the secrets of the stars and exploding the fitness myths. (Bet you didn't know that a jockstrap wasn't good for you. And we have some surprises like that for you men, too.) It's finding who the real competition is in a gym and learning how to out-dress them. It's how to choose a trainer; how to overcome pain, and how to deal with sex.

You can forget the baby oil on the biceps. We're here to lubricate your mind. And fitness, when you get right down to it, is mind over matter. It was Elaine Powers who said it best: "It ain't the meat, it's the motion."

> **YOU CAN'T START A FIRE WITHOUT A SPARK**

There are some things you should know here about Christie Brinkley, Jane Fonda, John Travolta, and Yogi Berra. Women and children first. The last time we saw Christie Brinkley, she looked marvelous. This was at a cover shooting for a major magazine. But come to think of it, if you had a crew of makeup, hair, and styling people working on you for three hours before someone snapped your photograph, you might not look too bad either. And Jane Fonda, please don't tell this to a soul, Jane showed up one morning at a very famous health club (not her own) wearing very dark sunglasses (did we mention that there are no windows in this place?) Now John Travolta—well, come on, if you only worked three months a year and then had all that time in between bad films to do nothing but play with Marilu Henner, you'd be none the worse for wear either. The point here—and you need to get this into your head—is that all is not what it seems. Very few of us are Christie Brinkley, Jane Fonda, or John Travolta. There are many ways to prove this. A small hand mirror is perhaps the most effective.

Getting started on a fitness program is not a matter of looking at some movie stars, saying, "Hey, I'll never look like that," and ordering another chocolate milkshake. No indeed. Getting yourself started is all a matter of simple psychology. This is where Yogi Berra, our favorite psychologist, comes in. It was Yogi who said: "Ninety percent of this game is half mental." Words to live by. They key here is not the math, it's the perspective.

You need to remember to be somebody unique—yourself. Don't compare yourself to movie stars. Don't even compare yourself to people who've been working out for a while. That's how a lot of people fall flat on their faces before they do their first exercise. They set their sights too high. And when they never quite reach those unrealistic goals, they see themselves as failures.

There's only one person you want to use as a real yardstick here, and that's you. You need to get a true feeling of your own worth. You need to recognize and accept yourself as what you are right now—imperfect, but changing and growing and eager to learn. It was Popeye who said, "I yam what I yam." You should tell that to yourself over and over again. And then you should eat a lot of spinach.

IN THE BEGINNING

You need to be realistic about this stuff. Sure, it would be nice if you could do 200 sit-ups. But how many can you do right now? Go ahead, try it. Put this book down, get on the floor, bend your knees, and start pumping. We'll wait here. Somebody has to finish the chocolate milkshake.

So how many did you do? Twenty? Okay, that's fine. All you need now is to get that into perspective. If you did twenty sit-ups today, then 200 is, at best, a long-range goal. A little too long-range, in fact. The future in fitness is now. And maybe tomorrow. But that's it. If you did twenty sit-ups today, your next goal should be twenty-five. And if it takes you a few days to build up to twenty-five, that's all right too. Arnold Schwarzenegger wasn't built in a day.

And neither was Maria Shriver. Fitness goals needn't be all athletic. Or all macho. Wanting to tighten your tummy after you've had a baby is a valid enough aim. So is taking a couple of inches off your hips or getting rid of that extra skin that starts to hang from your upper arms as you get older—the stuff we used to call teacher flab because it seemed most prevalent on women who wrote on blackboards a lot. Occupational hazard. Remember, these goals take the same patience and pacing as anything a real jock could reach for—unless you happen to know a good plastic surgeon.

Before you start a fitness program, there are some things you need to do:

- First, get a complete physical exam by your physician. Don't even think about putting on your sweat socks before you do this. You'll need to know your limitations before forming your expectations.
- Second, get a fitness evaluation at a club staffed with exercise physiologists or physical therapists. Don't just let the "manager" look you over. Last month he might have been selling aluminum siding. This evaluation should include a reasonable stress test, especially if you're over thirty-five, or if you smoke, or if you're carrying some extra baggage.
- And third, with the help of someone at that fitness center, design a training program that's right for you. To do this, you factor in any physical limitations and then make a list of rather reasonable and specific goals. Being fit, however reasonable, isn't a specific enough goal. Doing twenty-five sit-ups is a specific goal.

HOW TO STICK WITH IT

Too many people drop out of fitness programs because they've gone into them with unrealistic goals. Don't expect immediate results. And don't get discouraged when you feel some aches and pains. They last, at most, a few weeks—the big question is: Can you?

Starting a fitness program can be intimidating from the

start. Everyone else seems to be in better shape than you. And they all seem to know what they're doing on those machines. That's just a simple matter of experience. Like any new job, the longer you work, the more you'll know. You can't let yourself get discouraged when you feel like the one Rockette who's out of sync. It's a matter of swallowing your ego a bit for that first session and learning from history. You went through this same feeling of panic way back on your first day of kindergarten. Remember? "How will the bus know to pick me up? What if it takes me to the wrong school? What if all the other kids laugh at me?" You learned quickly to deal with all that. The bus didn't forget you, you got to the right school, and your older brother beat up the kids who laughed at you.

It's the early trauma of starting something new that makes it all the more important that you set realistic goals. It is very nice for Alberto Salazar to have a resting pulse rate in the thirties. But if your resting pulse rate is somewhere around eighty, a reasonable short-term goal is to get it down to seventy-nine. It works the same with weight loss. You might go into a fitness program wanting to lose twenty pounds. Fine, as long as you keep that in the perspective of a long-term goal. Don't expect to sweat it off the first week. A more realistic short-term goal would be to lose two pounds the first month. And even that's going to take some work.

Keeping your goals modest will keep you going. Most athletes, even the pros, will often make their first steps far too ambitious. The result, most often, is frustration. Take your basic weekend jogger. Maybe each times he jogs, he gets up to five miles. Pretty good. But then he decides to train for a marathon (over twenty-six miles). There's the first mistake. A ten-kilometer race is certainly more realistic. (But then, nobody ever accused joggers of being realistic.)

So, to start training for this marathon, our jogger tries to double his mileage. Ten miles a day. He might meet that goal for the first two days. But by the third day, the only thing he's likely to meet is a tube of Ben-Gay. He becomes too sore to train, misses a few days, and then has trouble getting himself back to the original five miles a day. Not the stuff gold medals are made of.

The problem of too much too soon is a direct result of poor goal-setting. To make fitness work, you need to continually plan a number of small steps, starting from where you are right now. It's the only way to get you where you want to go. Each step needs to have a high probability of success. And the smaller the increment, the higher the probability.

You might want to write your goals down. Some people are helped a lot by visualization. It's a simple routine. Just get yourself a pen and some paper (you don't need to put the warm-up suit on just yet), and sit down in a nice comfortable chair, and try to picture yourself at the next plateau of fitness. For a better mental image, you'll probably want to close your eyes.

A FEW WORDS ABOUT YOUR BRAIN

Painting a picture in your mind can work. You don't have to belong to est or anything. It's really nothing that cosmic. You know that built-in alarm clock you have in your head? Like when you set the old Sony for 6:30 and some little thing goes off in your skull and you wake up and look at the clock and it's 6:29. Well, there a reason for all that.

Somewhere in the middle of all the gray matter of your brain is a four-inch-long network of cells called the reticular activating system. It knows all and sees all. It acts as a filter for incoming stimuli, such as sight, sound, and touch. It decides what information is going to become part of your experience and what is going to be ignored. This is how people who live next to train tracks manage to sleep at night. Their reticular activating systems just tune out the sound of the trains. They teach their minds to play perception tricks.

The best part of the reticular activating system is that you can program it yourself to help psych you in or out. It can be very acheivement oriented. You feed it a successful mental picture and it will translate it into a positive self-image and a visualized goal—such as you doing those twenty-five sit-ups. And since you're probably not a pro athlete with a multimillion dollar contract to keep you going, there's a lot to be said for the power of positive thinking.

THE LITTLE ENGINE THAT COULD

You remember Dwight Stones, the high jumper. He's the one with the Mickey Mouse T-shirt who takes forever to jump. He stands there, almost in a trance, and moves his eyes up the runway one step at a time. Affectation? No, it's called visualization. As he rocks back and forth and shakes his head, he's playing one big mind game. He's putting his brain through the actual jump. Once he's ready to go, it's just a matter of putting his body where his mind's been. Because, as far as his mind is concerned, the successful jump has already been made.

There are those who would have you believe that the mind cannot tell the difference between an imagined experience and a real one, and therefore responds to what you think or imagine to be true. In such visualization, the mind reacts automatically to the information we feed it—real or imagined. So the same process that will get Dwight Stones over the high jump bar will get you to do those twenty-five sit-ups tomorrow. There are those who would have you believe that as long as you visualize your goals in increments, just out of reach, but not out of sight, you'll be able to achieve them.

Well, we're all in favor of the power of positive thinking, but don't psych yourself into the notion that your body can do whatever your mind tells it to. If life were that easy, Dwight Stones would have won a medal at the Los Angeles Olympics and you wouldn't need to read this book. As you'll learn, there's a lot more to fitness success than what meets the mind's eye.

PLAYING THOSE MIND GAMES

There are other mental exercises we thought you'd want to know about and try to avoid. One is called autogenic training. You find a quiet place, you relax in a comfortable chair, you keep your eyes closed, and you take a deep breath as you begin your exercises. Just one catch: the exercises are all done in your head. You just repeat a series of simple sentences:

"My right arm is heavy. I'm at peace. My right arm is heavy. My right arm is heavy. My left arm is heavy. I'm relaxing. My left arm is heavy. My left arm is heavy. I'm at peace. My left arm is heavy. Both of my arms are heavy. Both of my arms are heavy. Both of my arms are heavy. Both of my arms are heavy."

You then move on to your legs and then to sensations of warmth and then to your heart rate: "My heartbeat is calm and regular. My heartbeat is calm and regular . . ." Isn't this the way Christian Science started?

Now repeat: "I am lifting the Empire State Building." Come on. The idea of these mental exercises is to get you into a relaxed state. While we suppose this works for some people, we don't endorse it as an end in itself. Not that it wouldn't be nice. If you could do all this in your head, think of all the money you'd save on Valium.

While autogenic training is relatively new, history is dotted with those who thought mind games were the key to relaxation and the certain fitness that folllowed. In 1920, Edmund Jacobson, a Chicago physician and psychologist, claimed to prove that one simply cannot experience anxiety when muscle tension is reduced. Jacobson said that if physiological manifestations of an emotion were removed, so was the emotion itself. And, he said, you could teach yourself to relax tense muscles. He put his patients through a series of exercises. First they flexed their muscles from head to toe, then held them at a high level of tension, then let go. Jacobson thought this was a wonderful way to relax. There are even doctors now who use similar techniques to treat the pain of cancer patients.

We suggest you look upon these mind games the same way you view covert activity in Central America. At best, be an open-minded skeptic. Just because someone tells you a certain approach worked for them doesn't mean it's going to work for you.

That's the whole idea behind personalized training. You'll learn more about that in the chapter on How to Choose a Trainer. Some people need to be coddled, others need to be prodded. Before you find nirvana, you need to find your individual needs. Just what do you want out of your fitness program? Your goals will help determine your approach.

KEEP IT SIMPLE

Just as you shouldn't overwhelm your mind with strange psychological ploys, you should take it just as easy on your body. A crash exercise program has about as much effect as a crash diet. It's probably even more dangerous. The only thing that rushing headlong into exercise will get you is an extra set of aches and pains. The only intelligent approach to exercise is a gradual one. Sure, knowing how to start is important. But knowing when to stop is key. Your body is the best barometer for that. Simply stated: If it hurts, don't do it anymore. Don't say, "Gee, I'm really starting to feel this in my back," and then hope you can work through the pain. Be honest with yourself. If your back starts to hurt, then stop. There are no medals for heroes in fitness. Just Ace bandages.

Keeping it simple is important for every part of a fitness regimen. When you first walk into a health club and see all those shiny machines, there's a great tendency to make a Chinese banquet out of it. Don't. Just take it one course at a time at a pace that seems most comfortable to you. This isn't competition. The idea isn't to keep up with the speed of the person on the next bike.

And realize, as you take on each new exercise, that it may well take a few attempts before you begin to get it right and feel the true benefits. It's a process, and processes take time. Just because you don't get it the first time out doesn't mean it's wrong for you. You'll find that the more you work at an exercise, the more it will work for you.

EVEN THE PROS LOSE THEIR LUNCH

When you're starting out with a fitness program, self-discipline is often one of your highest hurdles. Many people find that devising a schedule is the easiest way around that. In the beginning, you may want to schedule your workouts at the same time each day. If you just leave it loose, you're liable to lose it. Making specific appointments and keeping them is something you're used to in life. If you can do it for the dentist, you can do it for your sense of well-being.

When you're working out, give each new routine a time limit—ride the bike for ten minutes, then work on a particular machine for five. Never say, "I'll do this until I get it perfect." That's one sure way of really getting discouraged.

Which brings up another important point: Don't get discouraged about occasionally getting discouraged. It happens to the best of them. Arthur Ashe used to have seizures of fear before every tennis match. And it wasn't over his ability to win. He would say: "What if I go through the whole match and can't return a single serve?"

Bill Russell, even after many years of dominating pro basketball, used to throw up before every game.

Golfer Dave Stockton might have put it in the best perspective. He was once asked, at the start of the Masters' tournament, to name the player who struck the most fear in him. "Me," he said.

You can easily be your own worst enemy. It's just a matter of gutting it out and not giving in to the temptation we all have every once in a while—to stay in bed, pull the covers up over your head, and hope that it all goes away. To keep you from coming up with any cheap excuses for not working out, you should know that there are only four excuses in life that are acceptable. They are:

1. Your dog died.
2. Dead dog and loss of one eye.
3. Birth of a child (natural mother only).

4. You are marrying Sigourney Weaver in the morning.

Beyond those, you're on your own. Just remember, hang tough. It's a dog-eat-dog world out there. Oh, sorry.

A TYPING TEST

There are, of course, two types of people in this world. Those who own a Mercedes and those who don't. No, that's not right. It's true, but it's not right. Let's start over. There are two types of people in this world: the Type A's and the Type B's. This is not a news flash. A couple of doctors in San Francisco first "discovered" the Type A behavior pattern some twenty-five years ago.

The good doctors, Meyer Friedman and Ray H. Rosenman, were doing some significant work on the causes of heart disease. Their findings showed that less than half the victims of heart attack demonstrated any real link to the normally accepted contributing factors—things like smoking and diet. Instead, they said, most heart attacks can be blamed on the Type A behavior pattern, a pattern of complex personality traits including excessive competitive drive, aggressiveness, impatience, and a distracted sense of time urgency. Type A people are almost always in a battle—sometimes with themselves, and sometimes with life itself. And, usually based on a deep-seated immaturity. Type A's can be very hostile.

None of this is to offer you a review course in Psychology 101. It's to let you know that Type A behavior can be found at its best (make that its worst) right in your local gym. With sweat clothes on, Type A's are highly motivated, highly aggressive, and highly competitive people. They're very goal-oriented and fiercely attack all phases of their training programs related to those goals. With that, they almost totally ignore those parts of the program unrelated to their specific goals. An example: The Type A interested in building upper body size will almost completely ignore aerobics, lower body work, and stretching. He will, however, work like a fiend on his upper body (usually with little regard for proper form), doing multiple sets and attempting greater and greater weights well before he's ready for them. Type A's often get injured doing this, but that never seems to stop them.

They exhibit their competitive nature constantly. They're the ones who look like the cranes in caffeine shock. You'll see them quickly looking around, comparing the weight they're lifting to the weight of everyone else in the gym. They can usually be heard asking such questions as, "How far do you run?" or "How much do you weigh?"

or "How big are your biceps?" Never mistake this for true, caring interest. Type A's motivate themselves to work out by comparing hard statistics, not emotions. And when they feel they've won one aspect of competition, they find others to motivate them even more.

Type A's are very impatient in terms of gains as well as time. They can be seen moving around the gym fast and furiously, trying to get as much done as quickly as possible. They get their pulses racing with the very anticipation of exercise. They often have high blood pressure, tight backs, and tight necks. And they're almost comical when they're stretching. They pull and tug at their limbs in an effort to achieve flexibility in a hurry. Compared to Type A's, Gumby was graceful.

Since they're rarely satisfied by small gains, Type A's see each achievement as merely reason to push even harder. They don't feel pain, or at least they don't acknowledge it. And most don't really care about the specifics or practicality of what they're doing, as long as they're working hard. To them fitness means getting in shape even if it kills them—as it sometimes does.

Type A's always try to get more than one thing done at a time. And so, while working out, they rarely stray far from their jobs. The fact that they've gotten to a gym and are actually taking some time for themselves is only made possible if they can manage to appease their guilt about missing valuable office time by doing work while they're working out. They read the *Wall Street Journal* on the bicycle. They have their Walkman tuned to the station that gives the stock reports. We even know of one corporate gym in New York that has televisions attached to their treadmills. And trust us, these folks aren't watching *Dance Fever*. The sets are tuned to a cable business channel—all day. Business before pleasure.

If there's one major negative attached to the fitness boom (other than the rising price of sneakers), it's the development of even more Type A's. The idea of true exercise is to ease your mind as you build your body. Somehow, it's an idea that gets lost in the shuffle of competition and narcissism. Too many people have set a goal of doing more and looking better than the person next to them. And that's dangerous.

How do you avoid it? We could be like some women's magazines we've seen and give you a simple solution like: avoid stress. (Don't you love it when they tell you that? Avoid stress. Damn, why didn't I think of that myself. It's so simple. Thank God I bought *Redbook*.) Life, as you might have guessed by now, just isn't that easy. One thing that might help you though, which is the whole point of this chapter, is knowing the enemy. Know the enemy and you will conquer. We read that in a women's magazine.

You should also know that there are other types besides Type A's. Indeed, there are Type B's. Tricky little system, isn't it? Type B's make up the vast minority of the population, especially in gyms. They exhibit none of the aggression or competitiveness seen in Type A's. They're never time-pressured or impatient. Unless pressed, Type B's feel no real need to talk about or show off their accomplishments. At the gym, they'll talk freely about almost anything. And they'll keep an ear open to what others are saying without feeing the need to compare it to their own situations. Type B's are easily the most effective in workouts. But don't take our word for it. Take that empty seat over there at the juice bar. We'd like you to meet a couple of real people.

Barry T., Type A

Barry is a thirty-four-year-old real estate developer who's been coming to the gym for almost three years now. He usually shows up around mid-morning. "I try to avoid the crowds," he says. "I just hate to have to wait for the equipment. The way I pull off the mid-morning routine is by getting to the office at about 6:30. It's just me and the elevator operators. That gives me enough time to work through lunch. I don't actually eat lunch, of course. I come to the gym instead."

Barry takes his exercise seriously, always riding the bike for half an hour before working out on the Nautilus machines and free weights. He's never satisfied unless he builds up a good sweat. On the weight equipment, he'll always go for a few more pounds, even if it means sacrificing good form and safety. He's aware of that. And he's paid for it.

"I hurt my back pretty badly about a year ago," he says. "I was going for a personal best on the bench press and something just gave out on me. But I wasn't going to let it keep me down. I stayed out for about a week and a half and then came back strong. My back still hurts me when I do certain moves, but that's the price you pay. You know what they say: No pain, no gain."

Sometimes, thanks to his hard-driving business style,

Barry will put on a few extra pounds—all those client lunches at the fancy French places. But Barry has an answer for that too. He makes slight weight adjustments from time to time by living solely on coffee for days at a stretch. "I can live without food for a few days," he says. "And it's not a total food fast. I do put some milk in the coffee."

The caffeine rush helps give him enough energy to both work hard and play hard. Most times it's difficult to distinguish the two. Business is never far away. He listens to the business news on his Walkman while he's pedaling the bike. "This summer," he says, "I'm going to have underwater speakers put in the swimming pool at the beach house. That way I'll be able to listen to the business reports and relax at the same time. Isn't that great?"

Karen K., Type B

Karen is a twenty-nine-year-old computer software marketing manager who takes her exercising seriously, although she doesn't get to the gym as often as she'd like since her promotion. "I work hard at my job," she says, "but I like to leave it at the office. When I come to the gym, it's to devote myself to exercise entirely. In fact, I find it almost impossible to exercise and think about work at the same time. I operate best when I'm doing one thing and doing it well."

When working with her trainer, Karen never plays the numbers game. She doesn't care about increasing her weights merely for the sake of self-satisfaction. But she is pleased when the weights do go up. It proves to her that the work she's doing is paying off. She's sure, though, to never get carried away with it. Anytime she can't handle a weight, she says so, and, having given it her best, she stops, without any feeling of regret or guilt.

Karen does take great pride in her appearance. "I finally lost the five pounds that have been plaguing me for two years," she says. "I did it all through solid diet and exercise. And then I splurged. I went out and treated myself to a new wardrobe of leotards and sweatpants."

During a workout, Karen listens very carefully to her trainer. He has her full attention. She's always patient about new goals, never hurries through an exercise or routine and displays almost no nervous energy. She concentrates fully on the task at hand and works to her maximum. "I'm under a lot of pressure every day at work," she says. "The gym has become the one place I can go to work it out of my system for good."

Clearly, Karen is much more in control of her life than Barry. So? Barry has no options, right? Once a Type A always a Type A? Not really. The doctors who first labeled the Type A traits have also noticed a definite change in behavior of some of their Type A patients. Some of those who've managed to survive the heart attacks have used the major warnings to reevaluate their lives. Many no longer seem as harried. They don't get upset if they can't do two things at the same time. And they manage to maintain a sense of perspective about life's little murders—like waiting in line or getting stuck in traffic. Having come so close to death, they have a new appreciation for life. The message here is simple. The smart people get a grip on life before it gets a grip on them.

But how do you know if you're a Type A or a Type B? By this point in the chapter, most of you have probably figured it out. Just in case you're still in doubt, though, we offer the following foolproof test. You should take it if you're not sure. What the hell, you should take it even if you are sure. Just pretend this is a women's magazine.

THE TEST ITSELF

(Make sure to circle your answers in pen. This will greatly cut into the pass-along rate for this book and mean more money for the authors, both of whom are Type A's and worried about their security.)

1. Do you have intimate knowledge of the exercise programs of:
- a) Yourself.
- b) You and one other person.
- c) You and two or three other people.
- d) Every member of the 1984 Chinese Olympic team.

2. You're sitting in traffic. The light turns green. The woman in the car in front of you doesn't move immediately. Would you:
- a) Just listen to the radio and wait patiently.
- b) Give her a polite toot.
- c) Stand on the horn and curse out the window.
- d) Hack her to death with a kitchen knife.

3. Business at the gym. Do you:
   a) Forget about work completely when you're working out.
   b) Discuss business occasionally.
   c) Ask them to turn off the Muzak and put on the stock reports.
   d) Know the numbers of every pay phone on the premises by heart.
4. On Friday afternoon, your boss tells you he wants to see your report on his desk first thing Monday. You work all weekend to finish it, but when you come in Monday, you find out he's taken the day off. Do you:
   a) Say it's okay, at least you got it done.
   b) Mumble vague obscenities under your breath but smile on the outside.
   c) Close your door and scream.
   d) Roll the report really tight and shove it up the tail pipe of his Jaguar.
5. Guilt in the gym. Do you:
   a) Never feel guilty about working out, no matter how much time it takes.
   b) Feel guilty if you work out, take a steam bath and massage without thinking about business.
   c) Feel guilty if you haven't at least looked over the business section while riding the stationary bike.
   d) Feel guilty if you haven't acquired CBS by the time you hit the showers.
6. After too long a wait in a restaurant, the steak you ordered rare comes out well-done. Do you:
   a) Assertively send it back.
   b) Don't leave a tip.

    c) Refuse to pay the check and steal a better raincoat on the way out.
    d) Look at your food and, in a very loud voice, say: "Ooooo, what are these long things, rat hairs?"

7. How quickly do you get through your normal workout?
    a) As long as it takes to read this book.
    b) As long as it takes to read this chapter.
    c) As long as it takes to read this page.
    d) As long as it takes to r

8. Your mother-in-law, the one who hates you for taking her child away, is planning to spend a week with you. Do you:
    a) Forgive, forget, and welcome her.
    b) Plan most of your activities around her.
    c) Send her the room rates for a local motel with waterbeds and dirty movies.
    d) Threaten to hold her grandchildren hostage until she leaves.

9. How long can you comfortably wait for a piece of exercise equipment?
    a) As long as it takes.
    b) Up to five minutes.
    c) Up to five seconds.
    d) As long as it takes to throw the bum off.

10. You hail a taxi (not applicable in Los Angeles). Just as it stops, a man runs up and jumps in, stealing your cab. Do you:
    a) Let him go.
    b) Tell him you hailed the cab first and he's very rude.
    c) Jump in the cab with him and refuse to get out.

d) Hack him to death with a kitchen knife.
11. You're spending your first night with a new paramour. In the middle of lovemaking, the phone rings. Your date answers it and proceeds to talk for quite awhile to what sounds like an ex-lover. Do you:
   a) Yawn, relax, and wait for the conversation to end.
   b) Tug at the phone cord and look neglected.
   c) Get up and leave.
   d) Decide not to tell this person about your recent bout with herpes.
12. How competitive and critical are you?
   a) Not at all. Live and let live.
   b) Somewhat competitive. Will offer criticism when asked.
   c) Very competitive. Will criticize any place, any time. Often in writing.
   d) "I'll make up my own test, thank you."

HOW TO SCORE

First, put on your best clothes and get a good seat at the bar. No, that's something else. Let's see, why don't you give yourself four points for every "a" answer, three points for every "b," and so on. Now, if you scored between thirty-seven and forty-eight, you will live long and prosper. If you scored between twenty-five and thirty-six, you have a reasonable sense of self-worth as well as a realistic knowledge of right and wrong. You probably won't have a heart attack, but you'll never successfully run for elective office. If you scored between thirteen and twenty-four, you should read this chapter over again. This time, try not to move your lips as much. And if you scored twelve . . . say, can we interest you in this lovely set of kitchen knives?

PSYCHING UP

We know, we know. You realize now that you should be working out, but you just can't find the time. Or you just can't get yourself started. At seven in the morning, the thought of lying in bed for another hour is a lot more appealing than busting your hump at the gym. Well, you're not alone. Even the pros sing the blues.

Take Darryl Dawkins. There are some days when the New Jersey Nets wish you would. Dawkins, who gets paid about a million bucks a year to be in good enough shape to be able to dunk a basketball a dozen times a night, has always had trouble staying in shape. This has lead to a number of injuries and to a continuing weight problem. So what does Dawkins do about it? Nothing. When it comes to psyching himself up for exercise, he's as lazy as you are. Maybe worse. The Nets management pleaded with him to go to a personal training gym in New York to try to lose some weight and get himself in better shape. Dawkins refused. He couldn't be bothered. It was too much trouble. The Nets even offered to take him to the gym in a limo. No way. Dawkins had better things to do— like sleeping and eating.

This, of course, isn't a smart thing for a professional athlete to do. And Dawkins isn't the first one to do it. A few years back, Sparky Lyle, then a Yankee pitcher, had the same problem. He was lazy, out of shape, and needed to lose a good twenty-five pounds. For a pro with a big contract, that's suicide. So why did he let himself get that way? Lyle's frame of reference for training was a series of coaches starting back in his Little League days. Well-intentioned men, yes, but not very educated in physical or mental training. For the most part, their idea of working out was doing a hundred sit-ups and then taking a dozen laps. It's no wonder that Lyle put training right up there with elective dentistry. Who needed to be miserable?

But Lyle, unlike Dawkins, was at least willing to listen to reason. He showed up at the Sports Training Institute to see if a good health club was really any better than a bad gym class. And Lyle was very surprised. The routine planned for him was anything but miserable. He started out easily by riding a stationary bike and then putting in about fifteen minutes on the Nautilus machines. It was painless. The routine increased gradually, but only when Lyle's trainer thought he was ready for it—both physically and, more important, mentally. The new outlook added years to his career and gave a whole new meaning to psyching up.

It might have all started with Ronald Reagan. Win one for the Gipper, and all that. In those days, psyching up meant a lot of screaming and banging of heads against lockers. Over the years, it got worse. Vomiting was added to the ritual. Nice touch, eh?

This foolishly macho system of psyching up was designed to raise the athlete's adrenaline level by initiating the "fight or flight" response. After all these years, some folks are finally starting to realize that there are some problems with that. First, when the body is placed under this sort of artificially induced stress, it produces a class of hormones called catecholamines. And these catecholamines get your motor going all right. Right into the red. They kill healthy cells and trigger heart attacks.

Scary enough, but what does this have to do with you? Too many people (Darryl Dawkins and maybe you) apply the "fight or flight" approach to training. It's all or nothing, right? No. Medical researchers have found that those killer catecholamines can also be released by overtraining. And overtraining is often a product of overpsyching. So forget every gym teacher or coach you ever had. The old methods of psyching up are just that—old methods. Current thought favors stress reduction and conservation of energy. Low-key mental preparation is what will get you to the gym and have you doing well once you're there.

GETTING THERE

There are a number of psychological factors that prevent a lot of people from starting or sticking with an exercise program. They include:

Fear of change. This has nothing to do with your socks. It's a little more cosmic than that. Change in any form causes stress. A new job, a new relationship, a new you. Wow, what's going to happen if you make yourself more attractive through exercise? You might have to deal with people socially and sexually in a whole different way. And that's serious stress.

Guilt. In real life, there is no such thing as one hundred and one percent. So if your dance card is already full, you're going to have to rearrange priorities. Rob Peter, pay Paul. Ask yourself these questions and answer them honestly: Can you take an hour off from work to exercise? Will your job performance really suffer? Will working out after work really wreck your home life? Is devoting so much time to yourself really selfish?

Intimidation. You think: "All those people at the health club know more than I do. I'm going to walk in there the first day and not know which way to sit on the machines. I'll be the only one there who's out of sync and not in shape. They're all going to point at my love handles and laugh." And you don't even want to think about what's going to happen in the shower room.

Had enough? Okay, now that we've triggered all your fears, let's try to tackle some of these problems.

First, you have to realize that it's fine to do something for yourself. It's not a selfish act. Just the opposite. By making time for working out and getting in decent shape, you'll not only feel better about yourself, you'll feel better about life, your job, your relationships. Taking a couple hours a week to achieve this is a good move. Walking after a golf ball all day Sunday, now *that's* selfish.

Second, make sure you give exercise a fair chance. It's sort of like brussels sprouts. You can't just put it in your mouth, chew it twice, and spit it out. (Actually, with brussels sprouts you could.) Just don't be that quick to judge exercise. Give it time. Make yourself give it a good shot. Set a time limit. We recommend twelve weeks. That's generally considered the time period needed for the physiological changes in your body to really get in gear. No excuses. You're going to gut it out for three months. Trust us, it's not as bad as boot camp. (You pacifists and non-Israeli women can ignore that analogy.)

Third, make it easy on yourself. Who sang that? Hmmm. Oh, the Righteous Brothers. Remember blue-eyed soul? Sorry, back to the book. The greatest danger in starting an exercise program is overdoing it. That's how you defeat yourself mentally. Also, if you find that after a few weeks you're not really enjoying the program, then change it. Work a different routine. Use different machines. Keep changing until you get it right. This is a good reason to join a multipurpose health club. If your mind easily wanders . . . "You never close your eyes anymore when I kiss your lips . . ." Wait, where were we? Right, if you're one of those weird people whose mind easily wanders, then give your body some places to wander with it. If running on a treadmill every day bores you to tears, then go swimming, or play racquetball.

Fourth, make exercise a habit. Get yourself into a ritual. Make it part of your regular routine—like breakfast or sex. You can play little tricks on yourself to make this happen. If you're not a terribly organized person, don't join a health club where they tell you to drop in any old time. You'll never do it. There will always be some excuse—you're too tired, you have too much work. You need a club where you can make an appointment. We find it easy to make it early in the morning when there's little else to distract you. If your only choice is between exercising or watching David Hartman, you're going to be in pretty good shape. (We just blew a national publicity shot there, didn't we? Say, don't you just love Bryant and Jane?) Another thing to keep in mind with clubs that take appointments: If you decide to sleep late that morning, you're going to have to pay for it anyway. You might as well get your money's worth. Cyndi Lauper was right.

Fifth, don't let intimidation get you. Only instant karma can do that. Just think about your first day on the kindergarten bus. All those big first-graders making fun of you because you didn't know where to sit (we won't even mention the Donald Duck lunch box). That was stressful, even a little scary, but you managed to get through it, didn't you? We promise, by your second week at a health club, you'll know where everything is, you'll know where to sit, you'll even start to get muscles like the big kids. It'll all work out fine—just leave the lunch box home.

Sixth, if all else fails, use guilt to your advantage. Sign up with a friend who's even more insecure about it than you. The two of you going together will make for positive reinforcement. If you don't show up, your friend's going to be a little annoyed. Now would you do that to a friend? Better yet, sign up with your mother.

HOW STRESS WORKS

Now that you've gotten over the biggest hump, don't fool yourself. It's not over yet. This is a very big camel. The stress that kept you from going to the gym might well keep you from performing at your best once you're there. You can make stress work for you. But first it helps to understand it.

Not all stress is bad. Stress is what keeps us interested and motivated in life. Anything that gets your adrenaline going—whether it's an important business deal or being in love—is considered stress. Whenever you feel particularly gratified by a situation, it's the result of working with stress. The bad part comes when you go through too much stress. It begins to take its toll. It can leave you tired and depressed, burned out.

In reaction to stress, your body releases hormones that increase the heart rate, blood sugar, and blood pressure while slowing down digestion and constricting blood vessels. Not a pretty sight. And if you don't do anything to stop it, you could be headed for some bad territory—headaches, ulcers, heart attacks, strokes.

But there's good news. Lying dormant in your body is a complete defense system designed to counteract stress. Endorphins, opiatelike substances released in the brain and bloodstream, can decrease your sensitivity to pain, slow your breathing, and even lower your blood pressure.

Forget Valium: Endorphins come free with every body.

There's a little secret here, though. Endorphins (you'll read more about them in The Sex Chapter) are most effective through exercise. They produce a sort of natural high that makes you feel so young. It's that pumped-up feeling you get after a good workout. You'll hear people say, "I really got my adrenaline flowing on that one." That's right. But more importantly, they got their endorphins flowing.

A warning, though. Endorphins can be addictive. Seriously. Compulsive exercisers often go through withdrawal and depression if forced to lay off awhile. Don't sweat it though. Healthy exercise should be the worst thing you're ever addicted to.

FRANKIE SAY RELAX

Exercise, in addition to making you high, can do some wonderful things for you, if you let it. Exercise works best if you're relaxed. And you can psych yourself into relaxing by not adding pressure. Don't demand perfection. Not in the gym. A bad workout isn't the end of the world. And while it's important for motivation to set goals, try to put them out of your mind during exercise itself. Try to enjoy the workout for the sake of the workout.

Of course, there's no "right way" to relax. It's whatever works best for you. Here are a few trendy methods of relaxation in preparation for exercise that you might want to look into:

Autogenic training. A form of self-hypnosis that teaches

you to relax your body and dispel fears about the workout. You repeat things like, "My right arm is heavy, my right arm is heavy." This works for some. For others, it just makes their right arm heavy.

Tightening and relaxing individual muscles. Starting with your toes and working your way up to the top of your head, tighten individual muscles and then, starting at the bottom again, relax them. This could help you locate places where tension is stored.

Imaging or visualization. You imagine yourself performing a successful exercise or routine. It's a mental rehearsal that helps relax your muscles for a physical task.

Meditation. You know. Contemplating your navel. Clapping one hand. But what do you do with the other one?

Yoga or T'ai Chi. Exercise programs that promote concentration, balance, and body movement. Very big in L.A. for the past couple years. But then so was pink tofu.

Ours is not to pass judgment here, though. Whatever works for you is fine. The idea is to get you motivated. As Olympic marathoner Frank Shorter once said, the toughest thing about running is getting into your shorts every morning. Once you've taken that first step, there's a good chance you're going to get hooked. And from there, the sky's the limit. Well, maybe not the sky. Maybe just the roof deck of your health club. We wouldn't want to delude you into thinking that starting an exercise program is going to automatically turn you into an Olympic marathoner. No way. But say, we do know of one job that might be open soon. How would you like to play center for the New Jersey Nets?

JOIN THE CLUB

Great news! Now you can look like Heather Locklear for only $3.98. Imagine that. You can have the same body as the star of one of your favorite cancelled TV shows for just $3.98. Well, it does say $3.98 a week here. Wait a minute, what's this asterisk? Let's see, where do you look to find what the asterisk means? Could you hand us that magnifying glass please? There's something down here at the bottom of the ad. Almost looks like words. Oh yes, it says: "$3.98 a week for 65 weeks equivalent to $284, plus $25 registration fee." Hey, that's over $300! And they don't really promise that you'll look like Heather Locklear.

They just use her picture here. The idea is you're supposed to think that Heather Locklear goes to one of these spas. Maybe even the one near you. "What do you want to do today, George?" "I don't know, Martha, why don't we go to that little health club in the mall. Maybe we'll see Heather Locklear." Right.

Look, there's a lot of stuff out there now. That's the good news and the bad news about the fitness revolution. Lots of places and lots of confusion. It's no wonder that the vast majority of people who join fitness clubs go three times or less and never show up again. The clubs they've chosen somehow don't meet their needs or expectations. And that's because it's a jungle out there and you need a good guide to help you get through it. Fitness, as you might have noticed, isn't just a trip to the Y anymore. There are health spas and yoga centers, health clubs and gyms, exercise studios and weight control centers. There are even still places called figure salons, for you women who still prefer to be called "gals." All two of you.

And there's so much crossover now (gyms that preach yoga; health spas that specialize in weight loss), that there's just no separating and defining the categories these days. Look, anybody can hang up a shingle and call a place just about anything. If you're going to find a spot that's right for you, you're going to have to learn how to shop. This is something like buying a car. A show of hands now: How many of you are still driving Chevrolets? Yep, that's what we thought. You'd better pay close attention to this chapter, especially those of you with the Chevettes.

A logical first thing to look for in a club is convenience. But that doesn't mean you should run out and join the one closest to your home or office. If only life were that simple. You must make sure it meets your major needs. How do you find this out? You start by visiting the club at the time of day you plan to use it. It won't mean much if you show up in mid-afternoon, see that the place isn't too crowded and then sign up for a lunchtime class. You'll have only yourself to blame if you can't get a locker. As a rule: most clubs are busiest before and after work and around lunchtime; Mondays and Wednesdays are the most crowded days; and things are always slow when the weather is particularly bad or particularly good.

When you go, try to get a feel for the crowd. Do they look like your kind of folks? Does there seem to be an awful lot of them? Overcrowding is the reason people give most often for dropping out of a club. And there is a crucial difference between popularity and overcrowding. As Yogi Berra one said about a popular restaurant: "Nobody goes there anymore. It's too crowded."

Clubs do have their ways of dealing with overcrowding. Some offer a better price if you show up only during off-peak hours. This is a bargain only if it fits into your schedule. Some clubs do put ceilings on membership. Find one of these and you've made a great choice. And clubs that stress one-on-one training naturally restrict membership through this format. They're also very expensive.

And, if you're looking for a social life in addition to a fit body, the one-on-one spots aren't going to allow you much cruising time. They're there for the exercise. If you're in it for the people, find a place with a juice bar, a large jacuzzi, and a big bulletin board. That's where you'll find the people looking for partners and the notices about this weekend's wine-and-cheese party.

How much can you learn about a club by its size and the way it's decorated? A decent amount. A place with a large exercise floor is liable to be very social. Or very crowded, depending on your outlook. Sometimes the best clubs can be the most spartan. And the ones with all the chrome and flashing lights can be nothing more than glitz without guts. What should you *really* look for when choosing a club? Here's a checklist you might want to take along.

1) Look up. Especially in the exercise classrooms. Is the ceiling mirrored? Usually something you only look for in motels with waterbeds, it's an important point in an aerobics class. In a crowded room, it might be your only way to see what the instructor is doing.

2) Look down. Is the floor carpeted? Does it feel nice and cushiony? Go ahead, jump up and down a few times. If you feel it in your knees, you're in the wrong club. The idea is to come out of this with body tone, not surgery. So don't even think twice about a place with bare wooden floors.

3) Take a good sniff. If the air is stale, you're in a club that has either poor ventilation or a dirty carpet. Maybe both. We know some people who've developed some very strange rashes because of unclean carpets. We'll spare you the details.

4) Check the weight room. What kind of equipment are they offering? For strength training and general toning, there's nothing better than variable resistance equipment—machines that change to accommodate strong and weak points in a movement. We happen to

think Nautilus is the best in this department. Other brands that get the job done are Universal, Paramount, Eagle, Hydra-gym, Polaris, Cam II, and Cybex, to name a lot. You see, Nautilus works with an odd-shaped cam, while others use hydrolic or pneumatic devices. No, no, don't start turning to the next chapter. That's as technical as we're going to get. We promise. If you want to read about cams and shafts, go buy a Nautilus book. There are enough of them out there.

What you need to know is that a club advertising a full circuit of Nautilus should have at least twelve to fifteen different pieces of equipment. Count them.

And while Nautilus is fine for general strength and toning, if you're more interested in body building, free weights (dumbbells and barbells) are the way to go. Why? Because free weights work muscles unevenly, which leaves you with shorter, bulkier muscles. That's strength and tone versus bulk. It's your choice. You can be Jane Fonda or Hulk Hogan. These are the tough decisions in life.

5) Check the aerobic equipment. A good club should offer a selection of aerobic gear for both warm-up and cardiovascular routines. Look for running tracks, treadmills, stationary bikes, rowing machines, cross-country ski machines, upper-body ergometers (oops, sorry), rebounders, and even jump ropes. A good variety of this stuff will keep you from getting bored and help you work around any injuries. Oh, and there's some nonaerobic equipment that you'll find just as valuable. Things like slant boards, dip bars, chinning bars, and hip flexor chairs. These do not include ropes that go to the ceiling.

Do they still make you climb those things in gym class? Geez, there was this little guy named Jack Cohen who used to climb to the top and then cross over to the next rope with one hand. And then one day he didn't quite get all of the second rope and . . . no, you probably haven't eaten yet.

6) Get your feet wet. Pools at urban health clubs tend to be too small. If you plan to do any serious lap swimming, look for a pool at least fifty feet long. Otherwise, you'll always be in the middle of a turn. And take a close look around the pool. Notice any scum? Besides the guy with all the gold chains around his neck. Scum or foam means the filtration system isn't working right. This is not a good sign.

7) Go to court. If the club has racquetball, tennis, squash, or handball courts, check the surfaces, the walls, and especially the ventilation. You don't want your goggles fogging in the middle of a too-hot match. And be sure to find out about added charges and availability of courts. That's one of the great health club scams. When they advertise "six racquetball courts at your disposal," it often means you have to get on a waiting list and then pay through the nose. "Of course we said courts were included in the price of a membership. But we never said you could use them."

8) Look at lockers. Locker rooms should be clean as a whistle. So should showers. Accept nothing less. Ask about renting a private locker to store your gym shoes and toilet stuff between workouts. Just don't leave your gym shorts and T-shirt there. Promise us that. And make sure the regular lockers are big enough. If you'll be coming to

the club in a business suit or dress, you'll want them to hang without wrinkling. So check for hangers. An Armani suit doesn't hang well on a hook. Also, find out if the towels are free. If for some reason they're not, you're going to have to add it into your total cost. And while you're in the locker room, make sure they have hair dryers. This is not just a styling tip. You shouldn't go out with a wet head. (I got it in for you, Mom.)

9) Ask yourself: Do you really need spa facilities? Steam rooms, saunas, whirlpools, and eucalyptus rooms are all cute. But really, you'll get the same effect from a nice hot bath. So how important are these added extras to you? And we mean added. Don't think for a minute you won't be paying for this stuff. And, if you're looking for a hard exercise and a quick getaway, you can probably do without the tanning machines.

10) Is there a juice bar, a restaurant, lounges? If you like to socialize as well as sweat, these are important. Do the people look like they're having a good time? Does the menu look appealing? How about the people?

11) Get personal. Most clubs advertise personalized training. But in too many of them, all that means is giving you the right seat height on the equipment. You should look for a club that will put you through a full and personalized evaluation. This means a body structure examination, strength and flexibility tests, and body fat measurement. Make sure they do this in a private room, especially the fat part.

12) Scout the staff. Are they courteous? Are they qualified? There are agencies that give tests to certify trainers, but the practice is by no means widespread. Ask

questions about this. Does the club require its instructors to have a certain educational background? What sort of in-house training program are they required to take? Trainers should have a good knowledge of both your body and the equipment they're putting it on. Good training will usually add a few bucks to the bill, but you'll pay for bad training in the end. And the neck and the back. . . .

BRAWN IN THE U.S.A.— THE FIFTY TOP CLUBS IN AMERICA

All right. So now you know what to look for. But where do you look? Follow us. We present here a lightning tour of America's fitness centers. We've actually visited and worked out in many of these. And we've put together a pretty impressive corps of workout warriors to check out the clubs we couldn't get to. These listings represent a decent sampling of what's out there. But they're just that—a sampling. This ain't the *Good Housekeeping* seal, folks, just a well-traveled, well-researched guide. While these listings are up-to-date as this book goes to press (let's see, it's 2:30 on Tuesday), the fitness business is very fickle. So you might want to call these clubs before you go visit them, just to make sure they're still open. Hell, you might even want to call ahead to make sure that Philadelphia is still open.

A few words first on our rating system. You'll notice, at the end of each writeup, a series of symbols. First, we used barbells instead of stars (cute, huh?) to grade each club. You can assume that a club wouldn't be on this list unless it were at least decent. With that in mind, a one-barbell club is average; two barbells means it's good; three barbells signify excellence. To get four barbells from us, a club would have to be ready for the Fitness Hall of Fame. Note that there is a certain bias here toward clubs with solid staffs, so that if two clubs have similar equipment and ambiance, the one offering good personal trainers will rate higher.

The money signs represent first-year cost (often including initiation and/or evaluation fee). For clubs that charge purely by the session, we've assumed a three-times-a-week frequency. One dollar sign means a first-year cost of under $400; two-dollar-sign clubs will fall between $400 and $750; over $750, it's three dollar signs.

Our other symbols are easy enough to follow. The little racquet is your quick reference to a club that has courts. Check the full listing for specifics. The little suitcase means that a club will accept people who travel. No more excuses for flabby business trips. Note, though, that the rules for a travel visit differ greatly with each club. Call.

Finally, for those who want to have fun, we've chosen the most social club in each city and awarded it a smile face. Silly, but effective. Okay, pack your gym bag, here we go.

Atlanta

American Fitness Center. 665 Park Place, Southlake (and nine other locations), (404) 961-0474. This is a family-

oriented chain featuring complete lines on Nautilus and Universal machines. The recently added Morrow branch offers a junior Olympic-size pool, Turkish sauna, and steam room. A place for a good workout but not a pickup.
⇤⇥ ⇤⇥ $ $ 🎾 💼

Downtown Athletic Club. Omni International, (404) 577-2120. Fitness and business meet here. The bar is as well-stocked as the Nautilus room. It's a social scene with an indoor track, twenty-meter pool, and even a putting green. You have your choice between coed and noncoed whirlpools and saunas. ⇤⇥ ⇤⇥ ⇤⇥ $ $ 🎾 💼

Lenox Athletic Club. Next to Neiman-Marcus, (404) 262-2120. A high haunt for local movers and shakers. Membership here is reciprocal with the Downtown Club. A whopping forty-one Nautilus machines, heated pool, jogging tracks, racquetball, squash, basketball, sauna, steam, and whirlpool. Even a tanning center and a hair salon. The South really rises here. ⇤⇥ ⇤⇥ ⇤⇥ $ $ 🎾 💼

Sporting Club. 1515 Sheridan Road, N.E., (404) 325-2700. A monster. This club covers almost ten acres, very glitzy and a favorite meeting place for singles with money. There are twenty-five courts for tennis, racquetball, and squash; a full Nautilus center; indoor and outdoor pool; a track, basketball, volleyball, steam, sauna, even an outdoor hot tub. ⇤⇥ ⇤⇥ ⇤⇥ ⇤
$ $ $ 🎾 💼

Boston

Back Bay Racquet Club. 162 Columbus Ave., (617) 262-0660. Converted from an old warehouse, this is one of the largest and most up-to-date centers around. Weight training mixes Nautilus, Paramount, and Universal. A dozen racquetball courts, tennis as well as yoga, aerobic and weight training classes supplement the workout. A very social spot. ↔ ↔ ← $ $ $ 🎾 💼 ☺

Boston Racquet Club. 10 Post Office Square, (617) 482-8881. Keyed to eight squash courts, this club has full-circuit Nautilus, free weights, and aerobic conditioning, as well as an outdoor rooftop track. There's also sauna, steam, and whirlpool. Although it's open late, it's not very social. Most members do their workout and leave.
↔ ↔ $ $ $ 🎾

Fitcorp. 133 Federal St., (617) 542-1010. As the name suggests, the workout is strictly business here. There's Nautilus and Universal weight training and an indoor track, but the big draw is the staff. They're all certified exercise physiologists, very well trained and most attentive. Not a meeting place for the meek. ↔ ↔
↔ $ $ 💼

Le Pli Health Spa and Salon. Charles Square, Cambridge, (617) 868-8087. This started as a hairstyling salon and exploded. It offers aerobics on a specially cushioned floor, Hathayoga, and a full Kaiser-Cam II

system. But it's the little touches that really make the place so clubby looking. Fresh flowers and pitchers of water with lemon and lime slices are everywhere (including the steam room); and the lockers are made of finely varnished wood. A class act. 🏋 🏋 🏋
$ $ $

Chicago

Downtown Court Club. 411 N. Wabash, (312) 644-4880. Weight equipment here includes Nautilus, Universal, Hydra-Gym, Cybex, and free weights. Lots of good courts for tennis, squash, and racquetball. An indoor track and large, very intense-looking aerobic classes. A four-lane lap pool. A juice and liquor bar to wind down. A nice place, but they only give you two towels. 🏋 🏋 ⫸
$ $ $ 🎾 💼

East Bank Club. 500 N. Kingsbury St., (312) 527-5800. Ahhh. This has to be one of the nicest-looking clubs in the country. It's two and a half blocks of Nautilus, free weights, tennis, racquetball, squash, indoor and outdoor pools, a track, a sundeck, TV lounges, bar and grill, super saunas. If you like a singles crowd that doesn't sweat very much, this is your place. Bodies everywhere. The locker rooms are so large, they could use a bus. If there's a drawback here, it's the lack of enough staff to handle the masses. 🏋 🏋 🏋 ⫸ $ $ $ 🎾 ☺

Jay's Gym. 316 Michigan, (312) 346-0774. This place is small, spartan, and serious. If you're into pumping free

weights, you'll like it a lot. They'll teach you not only what to do, but what it does to your body. And some of the best-built women weightlifters in America train here.
↔ ↔ $ 🛍

McClurg Court Sports Center. 333 E. Ontario, (312) 944-4546. A real find. Most members come here for the tennis, racquetball, or swimming, but there is a small, private, almost-secret weight room as well as a big new aerobic area. Locker and shower facilities are as clean as they come ↔ ↔ $ $ 🎾 🛍

Dallas

The Exchange. 700 N. Harwood, (214) 698-1091. True to Texas style, the club is big. There's racquetball and squash and an almost breathtaking skylit track. A full Nautilus circuit is followed by coed whirlpool, sauna, and steam. There's also a bar, where you can take the people you picked up in the sauna. ↔ ↔ ↔ $ $ $ 🎾

Executive Club. 5919 Forest Lane, (214) 233-0123. The elite link in the large President's Health and Racquet Clubs chain. A two-level club that keys on aerobic equipment and Lifecycle machines. There's also an indoor pool, raquetball, and lots of coed spa facilities, including a Scandinavian cold plunge—which is no comment on the sociability. ↔ ↔ $ $ 🎾 🛍

The Gym. 13619 Inwood Road, (214) 387-3079. They do make them big down here. This is a mecca for free-weight workers. Barbells and dumbbells galore, plus the usual chinning bars and Roman chairs. A body shop with a coed sauna, the folks here really like to strut their stuff.

Plaza Athletic Club. 650 N. Pearl St., (214) 922-0110. A very social spot. Steam, sauna, and whirlpool are coed. There's a lounge, bar, and restaurant. Oh yes, and you can also work out here. Nautilus, indoor and outdoor pools, six raquetball and two tennis courts. Individual instruction available to members.

Denver

Gold's Gym. 1068 E. Bethany (303) 671-9586. A California transplant, this place traveled well. Designed for the serious lifter, they have every piece of Universal equipment ever made. A crack staff of personal trainers are available to body builders and power lifters.

The Gym. 7562 S. University Blvd., (303) 796-9231. The newer of two locations, this is body building at its best. There's individual instruction in state-of-the art Muscle Dynamics weight equipment. Plus an aerobic room with a thickly padded floor; sauna, steam, whirlpool, and sun beds.

Sporting Club, Cherry Creek. 500 S. Cherry St., Glendale, (303) 399-3050. Sister of an in-town Denver club and cousin of another in Atlanta, this is a good-looking place. There's Nautilus, indoor and outdoor pools, and tracks; racquetball, squash, basketball, full spa facilities, even a napping room for those who tire of the active social scene. ↔ ↔ ↔ $ $ $ 🎾 💼 ☺

Los Angeles

Biltmore Health Club. Biltmore Hotel, 515 S. Olive St., (213) 612-1561. You wouldn't think they made them like this anymore. Especially in L.A. No glitz, just ritz. With Nautilus, free weights, a pool, spa facilities (in the steam room, cold water runs over the seat tiles to keep you cool), and a juice bar, this is a top hangout for downtown lawyers and bankers. Limited to 1,500 members, they even supply robes. ↔ ↔ ↔ $ $

Gold's Gym. 360 Hampton St., Venice, (213) 392-3005. Muscle Beach starts here. The regulars are mostly hard-core body builders, about 30 percent of them women. Nautilus, free weights, and Quest Star water exercise equipment highlight this chic sweatshop. ↔ ↔ ↔ $ 💼

Jane Fonda's Workout. 369 S. Robertson, Beverly Hills, (213) 652-9464. Special pregnancy programs have been added to the regular aerobic workout here. There are also jazz dance classes, and a nutritionist on call. There are still no lockers or parking, though. ↔ $ $ 💼

Matrix One. 1964 Westwood Blvd., (213) 474-3355. One-on-one training here is very upscale. This has quickly become the fitness complex for the very successful. Stars and studio execs work on Quest Star water exercise gear. The stationary bikes have TVs. There's also tanning, facials, and a hair salon. ⇤⇥ ⇤⇥ ⇤⇥ $ $ $

Sean Harrington's Tech Fitness Center. 3859 Lankersham Blvd., Universal City, (213) 508-5118. While weight loss is part of the program here, the main idea is to get in shape at any size. Equipment includes computerized bikes and Nautilus circuit. There are saunas for men and women plus a jacuzzi. Membership is limited to avoid crowding.
⇤⇥ ⇤⇥ $ $

Sports Connection. 8612 Santa Monica Blvd., (213) 652-7440. There are four other Sports Connections, but this is the one where Travolta filmed *Perfect,* so this is *the* one. Complete Nautilus, plus Universal, Paramount, and more. Racquetball, aerobics, juice bars, you name it. The new push here is yoga as a fitness discipline. Since the movie, many regulars are starting to complain about the crowds. ⇤⇥ ⇤⇥ ⇥ $ $ 💼 ☺

Voight Fitness Center. 980 N. La Cienega Blvd., (213) 854-0741. Yoga and gymnastics are keys here. There are classes for beginners all the way up to professional dancers and athletes. The center has a cushioned hardwood floor and features instant video analysis ⇤⇥ ⇤⇥ $ $ 💼

New York

Cardio-Fitness Center. 79 Maiden Lane, (212) 943-1510. This is the Wall Street location. There are also three clubs in midtown. You only bring your sneakers here. They supply everything else, including socks. Professional physiologists (as opposed to amateur ones) have designed a very scientific, personalized system of aerobics and toning. ⟷ ⟷ ⟷ $ $ $

Executive Fitness Center. Vista Hotel, Three World Trade Center, (212) 466-9266. With Nautilus, Universal, pool, sauna, indoor track, two racquetball courts, and a very cozy lounge, this place is plush. Designed with the Wall Street biggies in mind, the most impressive thing here is the extremely well-trained staff. Most are exercise physiologists. ⟷ ⟷ ⟷ $ $ $ 🎾

Madison Avenue Muscle. 244 Madison Ave., (212) 687-8196. Super high-tech, this has become the current "in" place. (Let's see, what time is it?) Geared for body builders, it features the latest Cybex training gear. There's a springy aerobic floor, lots of stereo music, a posing room, and videos going over the treadmills and bikes. Very slick. ⟷ ⟷ ← $ $ 💼

New York Health and Racquet Club. 110 W. 56th St., (212) 541-7200. Oddly named, since only two of the five locations offer racquet sports. The Fifty-sixth Street club is the best equipped, with three classrooms and lots of Nautilus equipment. There are trainers to be had here, but the staff is made up largely of unemployed dancers and actors. Often overcrowded. ⇌ ⇌ $ $ 🎾

Pumping Iron, Inc. 2162 Broadway, (212) 496-2444. Formerly Broadway Bodybuilders, this is real macho territory. They're great on free weights and Universal training here. You'll see lots of pros using the sauna, tanning room, and posing room. Not enough lockers, though. ⇌ ⇌ $ $ 💼

Sports Training Institute. 239 E. 49th St., 752-7111. This is the forerunner of one-on-one training facilities. Workouts here are serious. There are machines (mostly Nautilus), a small aerobics area, lockers, and showers. All sessions are by appointment. Trainers must have at least a phys. ed. degree, and many have master's in exercise physiology. (Note here that the authors have a certain prejudice for STI. One of us worked there and the other signs over most of his paycheck for training.) ⇌ ⇌ ⇌ ⇐ $ $ $

Vertical Club. 330 E. 61st St., (212) 355-5100. Very glitzy and very yuppie, there's often a fine line here between workout club and singles bar. The equipment, for those who wait in line to use it, is impressive. Nautilus and Cam II machines are complemented by an indoor track, tennis, raquetball, and a very large aerobics area. There's a restaurant, a lounge, lots of spa stuff, and Gay Talese. ⇌ ⇌ ⇌ $ $ $ 🎾 ☺

Philadelphia

Clark's Uptown Health and Fitness. Franklin Plaza Hotel, 17th and Race, (215) 864-0616. A favorite gathering place for young Center City professionals who like Nautilus and racquetball. There's a small pool, an outdoor terrace, and a hot tub for two. Cozy but luxurious. ⇔ ⇔ ⊢
$ $ 🎾

Holiday-Espre Center. Old York and Easton Rds., Willow Grove, (215) 657-8500. When you first walk in, you're not sure if you're in a new health club or an old disco. The Nautilus circuit is surrounded with neon. And that's just the beginning of the flash. A very social club with lounges and restaurants complementing the track and pool. There's a sister center in Deptford, N. ⇔ ⇔
$ $ 🎾 ☺

Main Line Nautilus. 931 Haverford Rd., Bryn Mawr, (215) 527-2200. Workout pioneer Roger Schwab supervises a solid staff, using seventy Nautilus machines (plus new Nautilus leverage equipment), free weights, and an aerobic circuit. This club also specializes in rehabilitation of postsurgical athletic injuries. ⇔ ⇔ ⇔ $ 💼

One-on-One Sports Training Center. 1608 Walnut St., (215) 732-3208. The business people with the bigger bucks go here. Individual trainers work with Nautilus equipment, free weights, and aerobics in tightly scheduled sessions that include warm-up, stretching, workout, and cool-down. ⇔ ⇔ ⇔ $ $

San Francisco

Bodycenter. 1230 Sutter St., (415) 928-3205. Affiliated with clubs in L.A. and N.Y., this gay-oriented spot is very high tech and very upbeat. There's lots of Nautilus equipment and aerobics classes. Also a snack bar and a spa area with a cold plunge.

Family Fitness Center. 373 Gellert Blvd., Daly City, (415) 994-1690. Built around racquetball, this club offers a decent array of Paramount, Universal, Cam II, and Lifecycle machines. The coed spa serves the singles scene well.

Gold's Gym. 310 Valencia, (415) 626-8865. Much like the L.A. original, this gym is for serious body builders. Equipment includes full Nautilus and Universal circuits as well as the expected free weights. No spa here. Just the basics—weights, lockers, and showers.

Nob Hill Club. Fairmont Hotel, 950 California St., (415) 397-2770. A very exclusive and very personalized club. Training starts on Life-Cycles, followed by full Nautilus circuit and aerobic cool-down. There's also Olympic free weights for those who want to pump. Limited membership.

San Francisco Bay Club. 150 Greenwich Street, (415) 433-2200. A large and handsome spot for weight training (Universal and Nautilus), racquetball, tennis, and squash. There's an exercise room for aerobics and yoga, a gym for

basketball and volleyball, and a twenty-meter pool with lap lanes. A good club for meeting all kinds of locals.
↔ ↔ ↔ $ $ $ 🎾 ☺

Washington, D.C.

Chevy Chase Athletic Club. 5454 Wisconsin Ave., Chevy Chase, (301) 656-8834. A penthouse club with Nautilus equipment complemented by racquetball, squash, and badminton. Also, aerobic and flexibility classes, a full spa, and tanning room. This place can get very social. ↔
↔ $ $ $ 🎾 💼 ☺

Crystal Gateway Racquet Club. 1333 Crystal Gateway Arcade, Arlington, (703) 979-9660. A very large and pretty place with tennis, racquetball, aerobics and jazz dance classes, and full-circuit Nautilus. The locker rooms and spa areas are very plush. And, while there is an active singles scene, there's also baby-sitting for family folk.
↔ ↔ $ $ $ 🎾 💼

Espre Center. 11820 Rockville Pk., Rockville, (301) 984-6262. Olympic advanced weight training, Lifecycle and Nautilus machines here in addition to racquetball, squash, indoor track, twenty-five-meter pool, whirlpool, sauna, and aerobic dance center. There's also a separate women's gym. ↔ ↔ ← $ $ 🎾

Executive Fitness Center, Vista International Hotel, 1400 M St., N.W., (202) 466-4192. You'll find some of the

Capitol Hill crowd at this medically oriented cardiovascular fitness club. Cam II and Nautilus machines are supplemented by courses in stress management. You need that kind of stuff in Washington.   ⇤⇥ ⇤⇥ ⇤⇥
$ $ 🎾

Somebodies. 1070 Thomas Jefferson St., N.W., (202) 338-3822. Isometrics, isotonics, aerobics, and yoga are key here in beginning, intermediate, and advanced classes. It's where a lot of high-powered D.C. women come to unwind. Sandra Day O'Connor tops the list. And you've always wanted to look like Sandra Day O'Connor, haven't you?   ⇤⇥ ⇐ $ $ 💼

PORTS OF CALL
Atlantic City

The Spa at Bally's. The Boardwalk at Park Place, (800) 772-7777. This sensuous club has the monopoly on seashore fitness. It's 40,000 square feet of exotic plants and waterfalls surrounding a full Nautilus circuit, saunas, hot tubs, four racquet courts, and personal grooming services for the highest of rollers.   ⇤⇥ ⇤⇥ ⇐ $ $ 💼

Airports

Air Vita. Dallas-Fort Worth Airport (coming soon to San Francisco, Los Angeles, Atlanta, Miami, and New York), (214) 574-2026. Don't you hate those two-hour layovers? Next time, pack your gym shorts. This flagship club, housed in the AmFac West Hotel, has a Versa-Climber, bikes, a variety of weight machines, sauna, showers, steam room, and even a nap area close to office space with typewriters and phones. You might well find your pilot here working out his aggressions against the air-traffic controllers. ↔ ↔ ↔ $ $ 💼

The High Seas

The Golden Door Spa at Sea. On board the Queen Elizabeth 2. A small, plush version of its namesake in Escondido, California, this floating pleasure dome features hydrocalisthenics, weights, bikes, jacuzzi, massage center, and solarium. They go through 500 towels a day here. Either it's very popular or these folks sweat a lot.
↔ ↔ $ $ $

HOW TO CHOOSE A TRAINER

It is, when you get right down to it, not unlike finding a mate. Except for the sex. (That depends on the gym.) But when it comes to working out, finding the right trainer or training parner might just be the most important decision you'll make. If chosen the right way, this person can be the source for most of your drive and inspiration. He or she can keep you going or leave you stuck with the dumbbells.

You should choose a trainer or training partner just as you would a roommate or a lover. You need to find someone you can trust, someone you can depend on. And you need to find someone you'll be comfortable spending a lot of time with. After all, your body is in their hands. You're going to go through physical and emotional pain with this person. You can't just do this with anyone. You need someone you trust enough to take you to the limit but stop just short of losing you. Think of it as light bondage and discipline.

Since personal trainers are a relatively new development (as well as a rather expensive one), let's deal first with training partners. It would seem simple enough to find a friend who will help you along and share the experience with you. But it's not.

Most often, the choice of a training partner is made before you even walk into a health club. It might be the first friend who says, "Look at us. Don't you think it's time we do something about these bellies?" (If this person doesn't include himself in the belly motivation group, he's probably not a true friend. At least not someone you'd want to chew the fat with.) Another potential partner might be someone at the office who's just trying to be sociable: "Why don't you come to my club with me? You'll love it!" This is your first chance to go wrong. This is where you have to stop and take a good look at the person in front of you. Then ask yourself the following questions:

Do I really want to spend any more time with this person than I have to? If the two of you are just catching a class together, this might not be a life-or-death question. Not much talking goes on during an aerobics class. But if you're going to do some serious weight training together, you sure as hell better be certain you can stand this person. Before you jump feet first into training together, maybe you should have a drink, take some lunch, ask for references, see a college transcript. Is this a person with whom you'll be able to hold lengthy conversations? You don't often get a chance to find this out in a work situation. "How's the little woman?" should not be thought of as a reason for bonding. Your one salvation here is that no decision need be final. Joining a club with someone doesn't tie you together for life. Only alimony does that.

Why is this person asking me to join him? (You can substitute "her" for "him" here. Except for Lola.) If he's truly interested in your well-being, good. But this is one place where the Bible is wrong: It is not necessarily better to give than receive. If your partner is the type who constantly needs you to motivate him just to get to the gym, forget it. In fitness training, you get no points for being your brother's keeper. You might well find yourself dealing with a person whose motivations are borderline; someone who will make excuses for not working out; someone who will quit on you at the drop of a sweatband. You don't need this aggravation. If you can't find a motivated partner, you're better off going it alone.

Do you have the same goals? We're talking both short term and long term here. If you're looking to bulk up and your partner is more interested in slimming down, you're not a heaven-made match. If one of you wants a nice, quiet training program while the other is hell-bent for leather—you get the idea.

Are you a leader or a leadee? This is like schoolyard basketball. You can't both be captain of the same team. Somebody has to lead this dance. One of you has to take charge of a given workout. It's sort of like deciding whether you want to go to McDonald's or Burger King. One of you has to be assertive enough to speak up, take command of the situation, and recognize full well that the burgers are better at Burger King.

Can this person motivate me the right way? The right way is whatever you feel most comfortable with. If you need positive reinforcement, you need a partner who, every so often, will tell you what a good job you're doing. Having someone who's going to embarass or intimidate you into working harder might not do it for you. This is what your high school gym teacher was for. At this point in your life, you might be better off with someone just a tad more sensitive.

Don't forget, you're going to get very close to this person. While he or she is helping you work on your strengths, you'll also be laying bare all your weaknesses: everything from that flabby stomach to that easily wounded ego. But don't let us scare you off. Your decision here isn't life and death. No, indeed. Choosing a trainer—now *that's* life and death.

CHOOSING A TRAINER

The personal trainer—the guy with the big muscles who gets paid even bigger bucks—used to be solely for celluloid heroes. Because celluloid heroes never feel any pain. That goes for their wallets as well as their egos. The stars of Hollywood would pay whatever it took to have someone come to their estate, tell them to do a few jumping jacks and rave on about how "mahvelous" they looked. Personal trainers, like alfalfa sprouts, became quite the fad. They became the gurus of the eighties. Raquel Welch had one. John Travolta had one. Jane Fonda had one. La-dee-dah.

But then it came to pass that certain wise people saw some real value in trainers. The right trainer could help you choose the right fitness program. The right trainer could help motivate. The right trainer could help you make the best use out of what precious time you could devote to exercise. So certain trendy gyms took the trainers out of the mansions on Beverly Hills and made them an integral part of their fitness centers—almost as important as the juice bars.

The logic was simple. If your Mercedes broke down in Watts, you probably wouldn't take it to the corner garage. Personal trainers became the elite mechanics of beautiful bodies-to-be. If a trendy club didn't offer private trainers explicitly, there were always those gym rats who would make themselves available for hire. And a lot of firm folks found that a trusty personal trainer, at an average cost of between $15 and $20 a session, can make a world of difference in a fitness program. But that's the good news.

The real trick is to find a trusty trainer. Clearly a bad trainer can turn you off to exercise for life. Worse yet, a bad trainer can hurt the hell out of you.

A personal trainer is more than just a training partner. Unlike a training-partner relationship, you're not just helping each other out by holding hands (except at certain gyms in West Hollywood). With a personal trainer, you are handing over the reins. A true trainer should devote himself solely to your interests and goals. He or she should know your body and your gym-psych strengths and weaknesses as well as you do. Maybe better. He's the one who's there to keep you motivated, focused, and interested. His job is to use his knowledge as an exercise expert to guide you into peak physical condition as quickly and as safely as possible.

But wait a minute. Before you run out shopping, you need to figure out whether you should really be in the market for a trainer in the first place. In the best of all possible worlds (this is not it), everyone should have a trainer—at least for a while, until you learn the ropes.

Remember the first time you ordered wine in a fancy restaurant? "I'll have a bottle of your best seedless red." You might have felt a bit ill at ease then. What you needed was a knowledgeable and sympathetic wine steward—someone who would have known enough to suggest that if you were going to order the filet mignon well done, you should order a bottle of Almaden Mountain Burgundy. And don't forget to insist on sniffing that screw top.

In many ways, this is what a trainer does—help you make it through the night. Should you have a trainer for a serious length of time? The way we see it, if you answer yes to any of the following three questions, you probably do:

1) Do you need someone to motivate you? Easy enough. Yes or no. If you're having trouble answering the question, perhaps this is a clue.

2) Would you feel safer with a trainer? This is particularly important for those who have injuries or those who fear them. Better safe than sorry.

3) Are you just plain afraid? You could fear the equipment or failure or not knowing where the towels are

stacked. A trainer might help you overcome these fears. A trainer is your friend.

This is not to say that a fitness program without a trainer is like a day without sunshine. It's more like a baseball team without players or fans. Call it a lost chance. Call it the Cleveland Indians.

How do you find the right trainer? That takes some real mental muscle. You can get recommendations from friends. It's a start, but a tricky one. Your friends might not have the same attitudes and goals for a fitness program—different strokes, different folks.

You really need to do some research on your own here. Find out what you can about the background of a given trainer. What makes him qualified? Says who? In too many places a trainer is someone with little training at all—just someone two plates ahead of you on the bench press. A trainer should have certification. If you want to be even more certain, check for degrees in exercise physiology. But there's a catch here, too. The market has begun to swell with qualified trainers who have little or no practical experience. Be careful. Having an oven doesn't make someone a chef.

And here's a big one: Don't choose a trainer by the way he looks. "Gee, that guy has great muscles. I want to look like him." Uh-uh. You choose a trainer by the way his *clients* look. Trainers rarely train their clients the way they work out themselves.

Once you've narrowed the list down a bit, hold off on a final decision until you've worked with a trainer once or twice. When you do that, try to find answers to the following questions:

Is this person intelligent? While there's not a lot of time for idle chat in a good workout, it's nice to have someone you can relate to on a verbal level. Unless you're Sylvester Stallone, you'll probably want something a little deeper than, "Yo, how's it goin'?"

Is this person sensitive? You don't need to find a new shrink here, just someone who listens as well as your hair stylist. You have your up days and down days emotionally and physically. You want a trainer who can key into those feelings and tailor each workout session to them.

Is this person attentive? That means to you, not the starlet on the rowing machine. This is part of what he's getting paid for—keeping at least one eye on *your* body. He should, at the very least, look interested. Remember, yawning is contagious.

Is the chemistry right between you? Instant karma's going to get you. It's easy. If the trainer's good and the chemistry is good, you've got a match. If the chemistry's not there but the trainer is good, wait for it to happen. But if the trainer's not good and the chemistry's not there, wait for no man. Kiss the bum good-bye.

Maybe it's because this whole thing started in Hollywood, but most trainers are good actors. The best can assume different roles for different clients. Knowing the script will help you a lot. Here then, for you casting couch pleasure, are the parts:

The Drill Sergeant. If you got a kick out of basic training or have a lifetime subscription to S&M Times, you'll love this guy. The most evident and notorious in any gym, he can always be heard over the din barking orders to his clients: "Don't you stop. If you stop now, we're just gonna start all over again. I got all the time in the world." Most gyms are filled with wonderfully sick stories about trainers like this. Like the guy at the Sports Training Institute in New York who didn't like the way his client answered him back, so he made him take ten laps around the gym. And the client, a top Wall Street broker, said, "Yes, sir," and did it. This style of training, while it does work for some, can quickly become tiresome. Not to mention humiliating. A competent trainer can be assertive with good results. An aggressive, bad trainer can be downright dangerous.

The Seducer. Here's the flip side of the Drill Sergeant. The Seducer compels you to do his bidding almost as an act of love. He'll never seem demanding. At least, he'll never bark at you. The two of you will just glare warmly at each other while he gently slips in the knife. At the end of the session, you'll find yourself on the floor in a pool of sweat thinking what a great workout you've had. The Seducer role often works best for female trainers. Daryl Hall works out. Why do you think he wrote "Maneater"?

The Psychotherapist. He draws the most from his clients by convincing them he has their best interests at heart and that he understands them, often better than they understand themselves. His schtick is sensitivity. He gets things done by convincing a client that limitations are all self-imposed. Given enough time, the client gets hooked, starts to believe this, and does more chin-ups in one session than he did in four years of high school.

The Iron Pumper. Often a jock who never quite made it,

he offers you all the glory of being a finely tuned athlete. He plays to the macho ego. Through serious weight training, he will turn your body into a temple. And the bigger the temple, the larger the flock. But real body building takes an awfully long time and works at a very slow pace. If you have other considerations in your life, like a job or a family, this guy is best left to Mark Gastineau.

The Glamour Boy. A pure exhibitionist, he'll create spectacular exercises and routines not for what they can do for you but for the attention they attract. He'll purposely pick the machines in front of the mirrors. You sweat, he flexes. He'll be the first to tell you that he's not really a trainer by profession. He's an actor between movies. Schwab's drugstore was torn down, so he's doing this instead.

The Expert. He read a book on this stuff once and he'll never let you forget it. Each exercise comes complete with long, drawn-out explanations of training principles. He uses the word "biomechanics" a lot and tells you that Jim Fixx had it coming. Those who can't do it, teach it.

The Lover. He's not here to work out, he's here to get laid. This is probably not what you're paying for. He's a pickup artist who knows and uses every line. By the way, lovers make bad trainers. Trust us. Great pects. Gemini, right?

If, at first, you don't find the right type of trainer for you, just keep looking. These days, fitness trainers are a dime a dozen. Actually, they're about $250 a dozen for a half-hour session, but that's another story.

HOW TO WORK OUT

You've read the books, seen the videotapes, bought the clothes, but what have you really learned about working out? Take a quick look at the books out there. There are the semiscientific ones—the books that tell you all the wonderful stories about Russian weight lifters. Then there are the celebrity exercise books—each with its own chapter on how to do a sit-up, as well as wonderfully retouched photos of the stars. Now get serious. Unless you're planning on wearing the red, white, and blue at the '88 Olympics, or if you're naive enough to think you can look like Arnold or Jane or

Christie or Raquel by the first blush of summer, you've been taken for a ride.

What you really need to know is how to find an exercise program that you can maintain for years; how to get the most out of that exercise program; and how to do it safely. You probably don't want to lift three times your body weight. And you should be smart enough to realize that true fitness isn't something you find in a week at Elaine Powers. Life just isn't that easy. Jane and Raquel and the others didn't simply design exercise programs to make them look wonderful for their cover shootings. They've spent years getting in shape and maintaining their physical fitness.

Getting there, you see, is only half the battle. Once you get yourself into reasonable shape, you're going to have to work twice as hard to stay there. You want a quick fix? Drop down and do a hundred sit-ups. It'll help you gain admirers and lose your lunch. But if you want to do something with your body, something really lasting, you'd better read this chapter.

There are a number of important things you need to learn about starting and maintaining a training program. First, of course, you need to buy a pair of high-top Reeboks. The other rules for survival in the gym jungle follow something like this:

Know what you want to accomplish. You want to join a club and get in shape. That's nice. But it's not enough. What do you really want out of it? What does it mean to you? Does it mean you want to lose ten pounds and trim two inches off your thighs or does it mean you want to gain ten pounds and add two inches to your biceps? If you've joined a multiservice club, it probably has the facilities to help you accomplish either of these goals. But where do you start? Do you try all of the equipment and see what feels right to you? No. The only way you'll get your money's worth out of this is to work with one of the experts at the club at narrowing down your routine to meet your specific goals. If your club doesn't have someone who can do this for you, you're at the wrong club. We don't care how hip the juice bar is.

Remember, you're the one who has to set the goals. Don't let anyone else do that for you. We've seen that all too often. Somebody joins a club and is immediately put on a Nautilus strength program. Great, unless he really wants to lose some weight and increase his aerobic capacity. Sure, he'll spend months becoming as strong as a horse before he quits, but he won't have lost an ounce or made running for the bus any easier.

Know what you're doing. When you first start at a club, you should be given more than just a guided tour of the sauna. You should be fully introduced to the equipment you'll be using. You should use this time to ask every question you can think of. You're paying big bucks here. You deserve answers. What does this machine do? What part of the body does this work on? Where should I be feeling it? Should it hurt? Should it burn? And how will I feel tomorrow? Before you start a single set, make sure the exercises you're doing are going to help you reach your goals. And make sure you're doing these exercises the right way. In that sense, you get what you pay for. A club with a lot of machines but few instructors can be dangerous. Turning your forearm the wrong way on one machine cannot only negate the value of the exercise, it can really mess you up. Beware of places that tell you: "Feel free to roam around and use any piece of equipment you want." Ask first, work out later. If you don't like the answer, get a second opinion. You need to gather enough information to decide what sort of program will work best for you.

Some folks find that heavy weights are the only things that produce changes in their bodies. Others find they react much more favorably to pushups, chin-ups, and calisthenics. Some ride a stationary bike or run to trim their legs, others find this only makes their legs larger. People are different. (You might have noticed that in the shower room.) The best knowledge you can have in training is knowledge of your own body.

Do what you need to do. If you cheat here, you're only cheating yourself. Your mother was right when she told you to eat the meat *and* the vegetables. A well-balanced exercise program is like a well-balanced meal. If you only taste the parts you like, you're not going to get the full benefit. Don't spend half an hour just working on your hips or your chest. Work on the other parts, too. You don't necessarily have to do them as vigorously, but (just like those lima beans that Mom made) you do have to do them.

All too often you'll hear people say, "I don't do leg work, it's so boring," or "I'm interested in making my chest bigger, not my back." There are a lot of dangers in this. First, injuries can be caused by imbalanced muscle development. Shin splints come from strong calves and weak shins. Knee problems in runners are often the result of good hamstring development and poor development of the quadricep (that's the front of your thigh). There's more to a bad back than weak back muscles. Weak stomach muscles will do just as much damage. The list goes on.

Besides the injury risk, there are aesthetic problems with uneven body development. You've seen enough people with great upper bodies but terrible legs. You don't want to look like that, do you? Look, it's fine if you want to concentrate on certain parts of your body. But do enough work on the rest of your body to at least protect yourself.

Work out hard. There's no avoiding it: if you're going to get anything out of your workout, you're going to have to hump it. And that means some suffering. "Going for the burn" isn't just a physical fad. It's true, it's true. The only way to work out is to do it hard. As Joe Willie Namath used to say: "Score if you're going to play."

Your muscles, including your heart, only change when there's stress put on them. If somebody tells you that you can improve muscle tone by doing lightweight or no-weight exercises, walk away quickly. High repetitions only work well with weight resistance. If you're not struggling a little by the end of a set, you're not getting a thing out of it. With high reps, as some muscle fibers fatigue (producing lactic acid, which causes "the burn"), smaller muscles take up the slack and start doing the work the much larger ones did in the early stages. And that, along with Wonder Bread, is what builds strong bodies.

If you leave the weights off and do lots of reps, you're largely wasting your time. With relatively few muscle fibers incorporated into the exercise, there's little muscle build-up. But with lower reps and higher weights (fewer times, but heavier), the more the muscle fibers are called into play. The more you strain to make the weight, the more the muscle fibers do their stuff. There are limits to this, however. We'll get to those shortly.

You have the right to say "No!" This is where common sense comes in. Learning to say "no" is not only the best method of birth control, it's one sure way of avoiding injury in the gym. You can say "no" to your trainer or you can say "no" to yourself. When? Your body will tell you when. You need to learn to listen. When working out, there'll be times when you'll feel an unaccustomed ache, pain, or twinge. When you feel this, your subconscious will start to click. It will quickly calculate the degree of the pain (the mathematical difference between "ouch" and "oh-my-god") and try to compare it to some other pain you've felt at some other time in your life. But the mind works in strange and wondrous ways. Before anything sinks in, you're on your next rep, and the new burst of pain has you considering every bit of physical activity you've engaged in for the preceding forty-eight hours. Still, you're going at it. Next rep. You're now trying to figure out at which point in the motion the pain becomes most acute, and if perhaps you're doing something wrong. Set over. Indeterminable damage.

What's wrong with that picture? Easy. When you feel the first pain, stop. If there's someone to talk to, tell him about it. But remember, you're in charge; you have the final say. That's why you need to be very assertive about your pain especially when you're working with a trainer. If it's pain, describe it as pain. Don't just say, "I feel that in my shoulder." Nine times out of ten, a trainer will say,

"You're supposed to feel that in your shoulder," paying little attention to your masked cry. That's why you have to tell it like it is. Simply say, "This hurts my shoulder." This will grab his attention, either out of concern for you or concern for the legal department.

Only after you've stopped should you assess the pain. It could be a fluke. Or it could be simple muscle soreness from your last workout. If you insist on testing it, do one more rep, but do it slowly. If you feel the pain again, stop, get up, and find the physical therapist. If your club doesn't have a physical therapist (and it should), get yourself to a doctor. While you're waiting for someone to look at it, ice the injured area and just plain stay off it. Don't try to "work through" an injury. Ever. It's one sure way to trick yourself into trouble. The increased blood flow of continued work can often cause a temporary lessening of the pain. That will make you think things are okay when they're not. A great deal of tissue damage can be done under the pretense of "working through it."

An injury isn't the only reason to say "no." You have that ache-all-over feeling? Feel real sniffly and sneezy and the other five dwarfs? Then this is not the day to go for a personal best on the bench press. Try to push it and you might as well put a sign on yourself that says, "Injury in Progress." No matter what anyone else tells you, don't push it. You're the only one who knows how you really feel. This isn't to say that you shouldn't work out at all. No, no. You don't get off that easy. But this is the day to say "no" to the heavy stuff and spend a little more time stretching and doing primarily cardiovascular work. As long as you don't overdo it, increasing the rate of your

GREAT GLUTS

A major part of good gym psyching is appearing cool in any situation. What goes into your body work is one thing. But what comes out of your mouth might be even more important. You need to learn how to talk a good game. And to do that, you need to learn the language. In a real gym, nobody calls a muscle by its real name. This makes no sense, but it impresses the hell out of people. And, when you get right down to it, isn't that why you're really there? Here, from head to toe, is how you should refer to your body:

Traps: Short for trapezius. Muscles leading from shoulder to neck.

Delts: Deltoids. Muscles of the shoulder.

Pects: Pectoralis major. Your chest.

Lats: Latissimus dorsi. Latin brother of Tommy Dorsey and/or the muscles of your upper back.

Bis: Biceps. Muscles on front of upper arm. More commonly used in swingers' ads.

Tris: Triceps. Back of upper arm.

Abs: Abdominal or stomach muscles.

Obliques: Obliquus externus. Muscles of the waist where the love handles grow.

Gluts: (pronounced gloots) Gluteus maximus. Muscles at upper back of thighs. As in, she's a real pain in the gluts.

Quads: Quadriceps. Front of the thigh muscles.

Hams: Hamstrings. Back of thigh muscles.

Gastrocs: Gastrocnemius. In real life, these are the calf muscles, but from the sound of it, this condition can commonly be treated with Maalox.

metabolism can often help in recovering from an illness. (And by increasing the speed of alcohol removal from your system, it can do wonders for a hangover.) If you feel you must do a weight workout, take it slow and take it easy.

Use your own weights. Common sense again. We each have different capabilities; different strengths and weaknesses. With this in mind, don't get suckered into competition with anybody. You have a friend who can lift a couple hundred pounds? Good for him. You do what you can do. Competition is for your ego, not your body. Too often, it will hold you back on some exercises and overextend you on others. This isn't good. If you want competition and fitness, a gym is not the place for it. Buy yourself some goggles and go play racquetball.

Don't kill yourself. One of the most crucial things to learn when beginning a new exercise program (or altering an existing one) is just how much to do. There is a simple rule here: don't do too much. While it's fine to "go for the burn," you have nothing to gain in going for the aneurysm.

Arthur Jones, the man who created Nautilus, states the case easily: "It is impossible to train 'hard' and train a large amount at the same time." Endurance and speed of recovery aside, the mere trauma to the muscles when working at maximum effort for a long period of time makes such effort almost impossible to sustain. Most often, pushing it to the limit brings too many other muscles into play to help perform the exercise. There's a danger to those muscles as well as the primary one.

You work out too hard, you're going to get hurt. Multiple or recurring injuries are your body's way of telling you you're being a schmuck about this. There is

GYMSPEAK

Here, along with a whole new meaning for juice bar, a glossary of hot gym terms.

Aerobics: Literally, it means "with air." Used to describe exercises that lead to cardiorespiratory fitness. These long-lasting, low-intensity exercises keep you breathing easily while keeping your heart in its training range (65 to 85 percent of your maximum predicted heart rate—approximately 220 minus your age) for periods of fifteen minutes or more.

Burn: The feeling in your stomach as you near muscular exhaustion during exercise. Caused by muscle fiber fatigue, which produces lactic acid, which has nothing to do with dairy products.

Circuit: A group of exercises or set of machines designed to work all the major body parts.

Dip: 1) An exercise for triceps and shoulders, 2) A gym rat who's a real wussy.

Juice: Anabolic steroids. Male hormones, natural or synthetic (yuck, where do they get the natural ones?) that have the ability, through increased protein assimilation, to increase muscle mass and size, general growth, bone maturation, and stamina. The most popular are Anavar, Dianabol, Durabolin, Deca-Durabolin, Maxibolin, Nilevar, and Winstrol. Cortisone, used in pain moderation, is also a steroid, but is never referred to as "juice." It's very hip to refer to steroids by name.

Maxing out: Going for your highest weight on an exercise.

Negatives: Those portions of an exercise that involve slowly releasing the muscles from a state

GYMSPEAK

of contraction to full extension. Negatives are usually done against higher weight than normal and result in more muscle stress and greater fatigue.

Overload: When the stress placed on a muscle is over the amount the muscle is used to handling.

Pump: Verb: To exercise with weights (short for pump iron). Noun: The state of having enlarged muscles from the increased blood flow during exercise ("to have a pump" or to be "pumped up").

Reps: Repetitions. Doing the same exercise over and over and over and . . .

Repping out: Doing reps at a light weight to exhaustion.

Ripped: Having a great deal of muscle definition or delineation due to low body fat content and increased muscle size. Has nothing to do with excessive drinking, except for juice.

Roids: Steroids. See *Juice*.

Set: A group of repetitions of an exercise. As in, "Look at the group of repetitions on that chick."

Submaximal workout: A workout that doesn't use one's highest weights.

Super-set: A sequence that involves moving quickly between two exercises for the same or opposing muscles groups worked to exhaustion.

Vascularity: When body builders reach a low level of body fat, their surface veins and arteries pop out at skin level. Men usually get it all over their bodies, while women tend to have it restricted mostly to their arms. Thank God.

nothing good that can happen in overtraining. If you find yourself getting injured repeatedly, it's time to rethink your fitness philosophy and reorganize your training routine. Other warning signs of overtraining include:

- Chronic fatigue.
- Persistent muscle soreness and stiffness in the joints.
- Staleness or general apathy.
- Nervousness, hostility, or overt aggression.
- Headaches.
- Dramatic unexplained drop in performance.

If you experience any of these symptoms, take some time off, see a doctor, and start to build back up very slowly. The whole key here is pacing. Marathoners never run full marathons in training. In weight training, "negative" or other maximal-effort workouts should be done no more than once every two or three weeks (we recommend the latter) and be followed by adequate rest. The same caution also applies to aerobic training. The soreness and stiffness you'll feel after a take-it-to-the limit workout will usually make normal workouts impossible for several days. Worse things could happen. Rest periods of a week or more often have a very positive effect on a rigorous training routine. So don't be afraid to take some time off.

One more rule of thumb: If you think you're pushing too hard, don't get a second opinion—at least not from someone associated with your gym. These people are paid to keep your enthusiasm high. Their motives might not be

GYM ETIQUETTE

You already know the most important thing: Wash your shorts at least once a month. But there are other, more subtle nuances to perfectly proper behavior in the gym. Here's what Emily Post would tell you if she worked out:

- Try not to ask the person on the next machine, "Hey, can I borrow your towel for a minute?"
- Politely decline invitations by locker room neighbors to try their new roll-on deodorant.
- Never stare at a woman while she's on the leg adductor.
- Never walk up to a man in Lycra tights and ask if you can borrow his newspaper.
- Never do laps in the jacuzzi.
- Never stick your chewing gum on the bottom of a machine for more than five minutes.
- Never ask the time from someone doing a bench press.
- Never take your shirt off in the middle of a class and wring it out. This goes double for women.
- Never ask another man to pick up your soap.
- Never go to the front desk with a bottle of shampoo and ask if they have any *real* poo.
- And never—and we mean never—block the mirror.

malicious, just misguided. So who do you trust? Yourself. If you feel like you're doing too much, you probably are. Remember, the idea here is not to kill yourself. This is particularly important in the long run.

THE GYM PSYCH EXERCISE GUIDE

The word "calisthenics" comes from the Greeks. It means to bore yourself silly doing dumb exercises made up by poorly paid high school gym teachers.

With all of the technology around today, you'd think that exercise would have gotten a little more exciting. But no. They can put it on videotape and add all the rock music they want to it, but a sit-up is still a sit-up and a jumping jack is still stupid. Calisthenics never were any fun. But then they weren't meant to be.

Actually, calisthenics started back in Sweden, somewhere in the nineteenth century, before MTV. There were the landowners and the peasants. (Some things never change.) Anyway, some of the landowners got to talking. They didn't like the way the peasants looked—all bent over in the fields, shoulders sagging from the hum of their hoes. So they decided to do something to improve the posture of the peasants. The peasants, the landowners thought, should carry themselves like soldiers. So they came up with some militaristic drills to try to perfect the peasants' posture. Sadistic little people, these Swedes.

You see, there are only so many ways man was meant to bend. Standing up perfectly straight isn't one of them. It puts too much strain on your back muscles and can be harmful to your spine. But the Swedes bought it. And they passed it on to the gym teachers (ever notice how many gym teachers are named Swensen?). And Jane Fonda went to gym class and married that ugly guy from California and made a videotape telling everybody to stand up straight—not just the Swedes.

And this is what brought us to where we are—a bunch of peasants spending forty bucks on a videotape so that a landowner can tell us to twist this way and turn that way.

There is madness to this method, but we're going to try to help you get through it. Look, if you're going to get involved in fitness, you're going to have to do exercises, no matter how foolish, no matter how useless. The trick, though, is to look like you know what you're doing. This is the whole area behind Gym Psych—to grab just enough knowledge to have everyone think you know the ropes. And don't listen to that junk about a little bit of knowledge being a dangerous thing. A lot of calisthenics, now *that's* a dangerous thing.

FANCY NEW NAMES FOR PLAIN OLD EXERCISES

There are three parts to the Gym Psych Exercise Guide. The first is to do the stuff you've been doing all these years, but just call it something else. Take a sit-up. That's not athletic. Dogs sit up. What you want to do is call it by a technical name.

"Hey, what are you doin' over there buddy, sit-ups?"

"Nah, these ain't sit-ups. These are concentrated abdominal curls."

What's a concentrated abdominal curl? A sit-up by another name. But now you've got them paying attention.

"Hey, look at this, Marge, this guy knows how to do concentrated abdominal curls. Like wow."

We'll call them C.A.C.s for short. You know by now that straight-legged C.A.C.s are things of the past. C.A.C.s should be done with the legs bent and with little or nothing holding them down. They can also be done with the feet off the ground and with the upper legs perpendicular to the floor. And don't lift the body more than halfway up. Beyond that point, the hip flexors become the prime movers, which is why your legs always tire out before your stomach does. Try coming only halfway up for a few C.A.C.s. Go on, we'll wait here.

Hah, they were harder to do, weren't they? But now

you've finally done them right. By the way, the C.A.C. is a somewhat overrated exercise. It's gotten the reputation for being the panacea for back problems. Not so. It helps, but if your back is tight, you should add stretches to your routine. If your back is weak, you should add other exercises to strengthen it.

Okay, now we're ready to move on to pushups. Oops, sorry, make that High Intensity Tricep Presses, H.I.T.P.s, pivoting at the toes or the knees, exercise the chest and the back of the arms (pects and tris, to you kids who've really been reading this book). A hint: pointing the elbows out to the side works the chest even more. And keeping them in close to the body works the triceps even more. Always keep your hands under your shoulders and your back straight when doing H.I.T.P.s. Letting your back sag can cause you to wake up with a backache. It also looks terribly silly. But if your back does sag, there's a Gym Psych way out of that one too. Tell those around you that you're learning how to breakdance. This move is called The Worm. Most of them will believe you. Especially if you spray paint them afterwards.

And next, squats. Now come on, can you think of a worse name for an exercise? Of course not. That why we call them Glut Busters. You want to shoo the flab from your quads and gluts? Who ya gonna call? Do-do-do-dooo-do, do-do-do-dooo-do-do. Glut Busters!

Glut Busters aid in posture and balance. They're best done using little or no added weight. Unless you're into competitive squatting. But that's too kinky.

Position your feet shoulder width or a little wider, with toes pointing forward. Push the hips way back, keep your eyes up, and sit back. Go down to the point where your upper legs are parallel to the floor. No further. And don't let your knees extend forward beyond your toes. As you come back to the upright position, the key is to not lock your knees out. And there you've got it. "I ain't afraid of no pushups." Glut Busters!

On to leg raises, now to be called Lower Abdominal Superflexes. Done with proper form, these can work the lower abdomen with little strain on the lower back. So here's the proper form: lie on your back with your hands under your butt, legs straight up with your knees slightly bent. Now lower your legs as far as you can without arching or straining your back. And bring your legs back to vertical. That's what they call doing the L.A.S.

EXERCISES MODIFIED TO LOOK MORE IMPRESSIVE

This is part two of the Gym Psych routine. You take a basic exercise and, as they say in the schoolyard, put a little spin on the ball. Like this:

Concentrated Abdominal Curl in the Pike Position. Sit facing a wall. East, if you're religious. Lie down and put your legs up against the wall and slide down until your backside is against the wall with your legs straight up. Put your hands behind your head and, keeping your elbows wide, raise your shoulders and upper back off the floor, leading with your chest. Between you and us, this is nothing more than a modified sit-up. But it sure looks impressive.

Concentrated Abdominal Curl in the Tuck Position. Lie on the floor on your back with your knees bent and your feet flat. Spread your feet about two feet apart and reach forward, extending the arms between the legs. Keep your palms up to add a little mystery to this otherwise simple sit-up. Actually, the form makes this easier than a regular sit-up. So you can do it for longer periods and impress your friends with your stamina, if not the cleanliness of your palms.

High Intensity Tricep Press with Half Twist. Do your regular pushup with one ankle crossed over the other. This is no harder than the standard pushup. It just looks cooler. Be sure to switch the feet occasionally. It helps the illusion.

Inverted High Intensity Tricep Press. Stand up. Put your feet about three feet from the wall. Put your hands on the wall at shoulder height and width. Now bring your forehead to the wall and push away. This is really a pushaway, done best at Northern Italian restaurants. If people think this looks strange, just tell them you're doing it to get a few more cuts in your delts. They'll understand.

Rectus Non-Interruptus. This looks like a pushup, but is really an exercise for the lower back and abdominals. Lie on your stomach with your elbows on the floor and your fingers loosely clasped behind your neck. Now, raise yourself up on your elbows and toes (come on, you can do it) and hold it for thirty seconds. If you find it hard to keep going, walk your toes in a few inches and raise your back a little. Just don't let your back sag. Because this is an isometric exercise (pitting one muscle against another), you need only do it once a session. But for those thirty seconds, all eyes are going to be on you.

Fist Wrist Lat Lift. If you can do regular chin-ups, here's a real eye-popper. Hold onto the chinning bar with one hand and grasp your wrist with the other hand. Now pull yourself up. This isn't much harder than a regular chin-up and provides no added benefit. But it sure looks great.

Up Against the Wall Mother-tucker. This is an isometric exercise for your quads. Start by standing with your back against the wall. Now slide your back down the wall, walking your feet forward until your knees form a right angle. And hold the position as long as you can. So easy, even your mother could do it—if she happens to be Elaine Powers.

THE STUFF WE MADE UP

And finally, the very essence of gym psych itself. Here's a wonderful series of otherwise useless exercises that we've made up to let you look like you know what you're doing. They benefit no particular muscle group, but they'll sure impress the hell out of your friends.

The Dynamic Tension Bench Press. Lie on your back. Put your hands at your shoulders with your palms up. Now slowly extend your arms straight up above your chest and shoulders, quivering and straining at an imaginary weight. Lower even more slowly, with a little groaning thrown in for good measure. Repeat ten times and sigh heavily to finish.

The Ilio-psoas Multistretch. Stand with your legs spread wide but comfortably. Put your hands on your hips and rotate those hips slowly, leaning slightly forward as you push your hips back and leaning well back as you push your hips forward. Do you feel it? Really? You must be doing something wrong.

The Leg Adductor Ultrastretch. Stand with your legs spead and your hands on the floor. Now bend your left knee and move slightly to that side. Then bend your right knee and shift your body weight to that side, extending the left leg. Repeat five times on each side. After all, you wouldn't want to overdo it.

The Dancer's Bridge. You always see kids doing this. And you never know why. Stand with your knees bent and grab onto your ankles. Now pull up very gently and look up at the ceiling. That's it. You've got it. And you'll never know why.

The Oblique Torso Twist (Again Like We Did Last Summer). Sit on the floor with your legs spread comfortably. (Notice how we stress comfort. This is important. If you're going to make something up, the last thing you want to do is get hurt.) Now reach one hand to the opposite ankle, extending the other arm toward the ceiling. Hold for ten seconds while breathing heavily. Now switch and around and around and a-up and a-down we go again. This will look very impressive. And do absolutely nothing. Trust us. Why do you think they still call him Chubby Checker?

THE GYM PSYCH FASHION GUIDE

Have we quoted Thomas Jefferson yet? No book worth its weight in pulp would be complete without a quote from Thomas Jefferson. Let's see. Here's a good one. It was Thomas Jefferson who asked: "Whose foot is to be the measure by which all our others are to be cut or stretched?"

Or was that Chuck Taylor? Those of you who still remember the days when athletic shoes were called sneakers might remember Chuck Taylor. His name used to appear on the top-of-the-line Converse All-Stars back when fashion-conscious boys and girls had four choices in footwear: black or white, high or low. But that was way back when there were only 200 runners in the Boston Marathon. Last year, there were 9,000. And it wasn't until 1967 that a magazine called *Distance Running News* could summon up 16 different shoes to test. Recently, *Runner's World* magazine tested 178 shoes from 34 manufacturers. And those were just for running. That doesn't even count basketball, tennis, racquetball, and squash. There are even special shoes made now for people who work out.

That last one might not be a news flash for you. You've probably bought at least one pair of fancy shoes yourself. What did you pay, fifty bucks? So, did they make you pump any faster or play any harder? It's enough to lead sensible souls to some serious questions. Are athletic shoes really worth it? Or are we all being had? The answers, unlike those old Converse All-Stars, are not black or white.

The components of early athletic shoes had very practical purposes. Adidas's famous three stripes didn't start out as a fancy logo. They had a function. They were reinforcements to support the foot. It was years later that some marketing type got the idea to color them for contrast. And time marched on. Certain innovations in athletic shoes weren't as scientific as the guys at The Foot Locker would have us believe. Here's one: Nike invented the first waffle sole. How? The company was started in someone's house. His garage was his workshop and laboratory. When he got the idea that his shoes should have some sort of patterned sole, he looked around the house for the right tools. What he found was an old waffle iron. Good enough. He put a sheet of rubber in it, closed the top and *voila!*, a fortune was found.

From that moment on, the idea, as the athletic shoe market started to boom, was to be different, to make one shoe stand out from the others on those crowded shelves at the sporting goods store. Maybe it was a wider heel, a higher insole, more nylon, less nylon. The key was that the shoe really didn't have to be good; it just had to be different. In the trade papers, they call this "good cosmetics."

Often the rush to get a new shoe on the market comes at the expense of the consumer. It's happened to the biggest of companies. Nike, which now dominates the athletic shoe market in the U.S., came out with a model a few years back called the Tailwind. In addition to being the first of the silver shoes (great cosmetics), it was the first of the air shoes; little tubular chambers of air were built into the sole to cushion every step, sort of the same way shock absorbers work on your car. The shoes, which seemed revolutionary at the time (if not in design, then in price—they sold for $50), turned out to have some problems. Some runners reported flats; the air somehow leaked out of those little tubes. The major problem, though, was with the uppers. They were made mostly of mesh—the next step away from nylon. But this particular mesh was a mess; there were complaints of tears and poor wear. The shoes went back to the drawing board, where the flats were fixed and the mesh was replaced with, you guessed it, good old-fashioned nylon.

And the experimenting went on. Some companies

came out with shoes that had nonaligned lacing. That means the holes where the laces go were staggered, supposedly to provide better fit and even out pressure distribution. Then there were shoes with two set of laces, and then no laces at all—Velcro.

And now come aerobic shoes, workout shoes. Science or scam? The manufacturers claim the outsoles provide more stability and lateral support than those of our old running shoes. That should, they tell us, avoid ankle and calf injuries. The midsoles are designed to offer good shock absorption and give the Achilles tendon a lift. The heel and toe wraps are there to provide increased stability in lateral movements. And the leather uppers should help cushion the blow when we drop the dumbbells on our toes.

What does it all mean? Are the shoe companies really making great advances? Well, some of them sound good. But, to be perfectly honest, you're hearing that from a couple of guys who bought Tailwinds.

Are specialized shoes really worth it? Do the gimmicks outweigh the good? Would we all be better off going back to deck shoes? Along the way, we spoke to some real experts.

One of them, Dr. Robert Brennan, a founder of the American Academy of Podiatric Sports Medicine, said: "Athletic shoes aren't just gimmicks. It's like having different race cars for different tracks. There are so many on the market now, though, that you should make sure you buy the right shape shoe for the shape of your foot. Unfortunately, many stores selling athletic shoes are staffed by teenagers. Try to find the more specialized stores, where the salespeople know the product and can advise you."

Good advice for those of you thinking of joining the stampede. And a stampede it is. Way back in 1982, an English company called Reebok came out with one of the first aerobic shoes. That year, the company did $3.2 million worth of business in the States. In 1985, Reebok's total net sales were over a cool $230 million.

And shoes are just the groundswell of the fitness-fashion boom. If shoes make the foundation, clothes make the man. And woman. It wasn't so long ago that men who worked out wore white gym shorts and women who exercised wore black leotards—a step up from the blue bloomers of their high school days. But then, as health clubs started to go coed, a lot of men and woman started dressing just as much for each other as for the workout. The mixture of sex and sweat brought some real style to workout clothes. And new fabrics brought new function. Some took away sweat, others protected the body from heavy heats and big chills.

And soon men started wearing gym shorts that were colorful and, we blush at the thought, clingy. Some men even started wearing tights. And women, well, they turned dressing for the gym into a real science—and a little bit of mirrored magic. Those who wanted longer legs wore leotards with high-cut leg holes. Those who wanted to make midriffs appear smaller went with nipped-in waists. Those who wanted to cover waistlines that weren't yet worked off wore blousy leotards with batwing sleeves. Those who wanted to show off their chests turned to skinny straps. And those who wanted to show off their whole bodies skipped the leotards and went with unitards—those one-piece body suits with the tights built in. Many found better living through chemicals, as nylon spandex became the cure-all fabric. It shaped the body by preventing bulges from jiggling when in motion. So much for truth in packaging.

Some looks were borrowed from dancing, others from real sports. The new gym clothes became a great new form of self expression. You can tell an awful lot about a person by the way he or she dresses for a workout. Any minute now, you'll get to our Gym Psych Guide to Workout Chic. It'll help you recreate hot looks in the gym as well as provide an indispensible tip sheet to fellow fashion plates.

But first, one stranger-than-fiction story we call:

The Woman With Two Bras

Carol B. is an advertising sales exec in Chicago. She works out a lot, runs a little, and is a big baseball fan.

"I read this story one day about Tom Seaver," she says. "It said that he wears two jockstraps when he pitches. Now Tom Seaver is a pretty smart man, so there must be something to that, I thought. Sort of preventive medicine. I'd always worn a bra when I exercised. I wore one with the straps that cross your back for more support. But I still bounced a little. I asked a doctor friend of mine about it and she said that once those breast ligaments stretch, there's nothing you can do. I got this terrible picture in my head. After all this working out, the rest of my body would be in shape, but I'd end up having breasts like those New

Guinea women in *National Geographic*. So that's when I started wearing two bras, just like Tom Seaver. You know what I mean. And I do notice a difference. I don't seem to jiggle as much anymore. But I still have this one fear. What if I faint and they take me to the hospital and when they undress me they see that I'm wearing two bras. 'Aha,' they'll say, 'that's why she fainted. All those bras cut off her circulation.'"

HOW TO WEAR YOUR TOWEL

You should give this some real thought. Style is everything. Try some of these on for size:

- *The Symmetrical Swirl.* Roll the towel around your neck and let it cascade to your chest. But be precise. A sloppy towel is a sloppy mind. Both ends should hit at the same spot on your chest. But you should never appear so vain as to look in a mirror to even them. Constant tugging should do it. Beware of neck chafing.
- *In Your Face With Grace.* This is where the towel becomes an extension of your chin. You roll it and keep it in place by sticking it in your T-shirt. There are two ways to do this. There's the understated elegance of the ascot look. But we prefer the linebacker neck brace version. It looks so wonderfully butch.
- *Stick It Where the Sun Don't Shine.* There are two ways of tucking your towel in your shorts. You can do it in the back like a center or in the front like a quarterback. In

> certain gyms these techniques are very definite signals in semaphore sex. Never mind that. Just don't roll the towel up and stick it *in* your shorts. This is known as the Mick Jagger look.
> - *The John Thompson Over-the-Shoulder Drop.* The ultimate casual style developed by the Georgetown coach himself. Be careful with this one, though. You'll gain the admiration of your peers, but you'll lose the national championship.

WHY YOU SWEAT

What's that you say—women don't sweat, they glow? Listen pal, sweat is a mixture of water, body salts, and acidic waste products. Glow that. Sweat is your body's natural air-conditioning system. While you burn the calories, your sweat pores let all the gook out. And men, because of hormonal makeup, sweat more than women. What can you do about sweat? Flaunt it. How else will those wimps know how hard you've been working out? If you sweat a lot, wear thin clothes and light T-shirts. That'll make it more obvious. If you only sweat a little, wear colors that will easily darken when wet. And you should always try to sweat on your chest. It makes men look tough and gives women sensuous contour. Just one more thing. If you tend to sweat in the crotch, never wear light-colored shorts when riding a stationary bicycle. God knows what people will think.

THE GYM PSYCH GUIDE TO WORKOUT CHIC
Women

The Gym Dandy. The kind of woman who cleans up for the maid. She wears purple V-neck leotards over an animal print Lycra top. She is cinched at the waist with a sash of neon yellow. Her shoes, Reebok high-tops, are the same shade of yellow as her sash. Her nails match her leotard. Her socks are E.G.s that bunch down. She wears large earrings. But, in an effort to look somewhat sports-serious, she leaves the second set of holes vacant. And she is fully made up. At all times.

The Princess. She wears little pink tights with little pink leotards, little pink ballet slippers, and carries a little pink towel and matching Walkman. Her little pink sweatband is worn over her ears. She never sweats and never works out in public. She just talks to others who do, while she adjusts her little pink leg-warmers. Everyone in the gym notices her Visible Panty Line. Her jewelry is still on. And we're not talking just simple pearls.

The Pure Pumper. Serious stuff. Her role model in life is Cher. She wears a black unitard scooped down below her navel. A man's undershirt torn off just below the bustline is all that shows underneath. She wears a double belt low and mean just high of her hips. Bought at Bottega Veneta on Rodeo Drive, it's much more motion than meat. The six-inch-long leather brace on her right arm was bought at a punk shop on Melrose. She removed the studs. She wears black Nike wrestling shoes with the perforated logo. No socks. No bra. Never let function get in the way of fashion.

Men

The Jilted Jock. He always went out for sports, but never really made the team. Never mind. The gym is his shot to strut. He looks like the winner of a five-minute shopping spree at Herman's, wearing every label you could possibly combine. A faded Nike T-shirt with Adidas shorts and Saranac wristbands (the kind the pros wear). The T-shirt, of course, is worn inside out to show everyone it's the second time around. He sweats and he's proud of it. When he goes outside, he wears his sweat pants *under* his shorts. It's a look. He wears a weight glove cut off at the knuckles and an old pair of Brooks Vantage, left over from his running days. And he always wears at least one knee brace. It's an old one. Try not to ask him about it.

Too Serious to Be True. He works very hard at making you think he really doesn't care about workout clothes. And that he's not new to the sport. All his stuff just sort of fell together. Sure. The very faded T-shirt with the cut-off sleeves says something about a 10K race in the Hamptons. Must have been ten years ago. He has peeled the logo off his nylon shorts. He carries around a professional weightlifter's belt, but never wears it. His headband has long lost its terry. He wears those unmarked, yellowish Spalding sweat socks that you can't find anymore. And, of course, a pair of Converse All-Stars once worn by Chuck Taylor.

The Yumpy (Young Urban Muscular Professional). His glasses are wire-rimmed and roundish. The preppy look comes naturally to him. His T-shirt is not really an item of clothing, it's his pedigree and résumé. It says Groton Prep, Andover, Yale, and London School of Economics. And that's just on the front. He wears gray sweat pants with a small crest of a logo. Faded. Underneath are his L.L. Bean hiking shorts, just in case. He would never let Lycra touch his body. The elastic in his anklet socks no longer works. And he's still wearing Topsider sneakers. He carries no Walkman. He just hums Cole Porter.

THE SEX CHAPTER

They used to call it the broad jump. In 1968, at the Olympics in Mexico City, U.S. jumper Bob Beamon shattered the existing world record with a leap of twenty-nine feet two and one-half inches. Some seventeen years later, the rest of the world is still trying to come close. What was Beamon's secret? How did he prepare himself the night before the big jump? With sex. Beamon had intercourse the night before. Hell, he screwed his brains out. He was very cool about the whole thing. Afterward, he admitted the sex, and his only comment was, "What do I do now?" Oh, a cigarette usually does the trick, Bob.

There's always been some mystery, if not confusion, about sex and sports. Different athletes handled it in different ways. Muhammad Ali always stayed celibate for six weeks before a fight. Did it help? Ali thought so. And it's hard to argue with his record. But for those of you, men and women alike, who are more concerned fighting the battle of the bulge than the heavyweight championship, there are some things you should know about sex and athletics.

Sex isn't all that taxing. Intercourse, even at its most passionate, burns up about 250 calories an hour. And unless you're going for a world record in the sack, it's unlikely that you'll lose more than twenty-five calories, since the average lovemaking session lasts about five minutes. (Did you ever wonder who times these things? And where do they hide?)

To put those twenty-five calories into a gym perspective, you'll burn off about twice that in your preworkout warm-up and stretch. For those of you not yet in the gym, it takes about twenty-five calories to walk up a flight of stairs. So if your bedroom is on the second floor, you're burning just as much energy going as you are coming. So to speak.

Some athletes fear that sex will ruin their concentration. Actually, just the opposite might be true. Sex, like exercise, is a good way of venting stress—of losing a lot of pent-up negative energy.

You have to know something about how the body works to understand this. The adrenaline flow, the heightened blood pressure—the same biological process that gets you pumped up for sports—also gets you pumped up for sex.

This is where the brain comes in. The brain plays traffic cop. Once the juices start to flow, the brain sends them to the areas involved in the specific activity. And since the body can only concentrate fully on one stimulus at a time, you're unlikely to see a man get an erection doing a bench press.

This bodily flow of one-way traffic also explains why after what seems like an exhausting workout, most people still have lots of energy for sex. In fact, while getting those juices flowing without draining the vital organs, the workout now becomes a very interesting and very effective form of foreplay. And there is data, dating back to Kinsey, that shows the sex drive and sexual frequency of an athlete exceeds those of the general population.

Lately, there's been some speculation about internal stimuli. You might have picked up on this if you watched the Olympic marathon. Some of the runners interviewed talked abut a mysterious "natural high" that comes over them at a certain point in the race. Some said it was like a cocaine high—you just sort of float along, aware of things outside your body, but not affected by them. The feeling is caused by endorphins—the generic name for any of several opiatelike substances produced by the body itself and released in the brain in response to stress. (Discussed in Psyching Up.)

When runners get their "second wind," when they experience that so-called "runner's high," their endorphins have been released. And it's not just limited to running. It happens in weight lifting and aerobics, too. The immediate effect is a sense of euphoria and a floating-on-air feeling that makes you think you can do anything.

This, combined with increased adrenaline levels, can turn the normally meek and mild into the superaggressive. Wally Cox meet Lyle Alzado.

There's a workout-related plus, though, that lasts a lot longer than an endorphin rush. It's called confidence. And it's simple enough. The more you work out, the better shape you get in, and the better you feel about yourself. It doesn't take a sociologist to figure that this positive self-image can lead to a more active social life, even to sex. Why do you think health clubs have been called the singles bars of the eighties?

SEX AND STEROIDS

There are always those who need to take it one toke over the line. Not satisfied with the body's ability to deliver a natural high, they'll look for a little help through chemistry. Enter steroids—male hormones produced naturally by the testes or developed synthetically in the lab.

The main natural male hormone (both sexes produce male and female hormones) is testosterone. In its normal function, it's what makes males generally larger and stronger than females after puberty. Testosterone causes the body to retain nitrogen, part of the amino acid structure that builds strong muscles.

And then there are the synthetics, the anabolic steroids produced under names like Anavar, Dianabol, Durabolin, and Winstrol. Many consider them the ultimate narcissistic tools. They're taken orally or by injection. They sort of help nature along a little by stimulating muscle growth through protein assimilation. That's the good news.

The other side of anabolic steroids is that they can shrink the testicles, lower the sperm count, cause impotence, promote male breast enlargement, decrease the libido, damage the prostate, alter the function of the liver, and cause cholesterol deposits in the arteries—which can eventually lead to heart attack or stroke. And that's just in men. In women, anabolic steroids can cause hair growth in some unlikely places; a permanent change in the vocal chords, resulting in a deepening of the voice; and, some doctors now tell us, a strong possibility of cancer. Heard enough? Good.

ABOUT IMPOTENCE

There are still those who fear increased physical activity will lead to impotence in both men and women (frigidity, if you prefer the sexist term). That's just not true. What really causes sexual inadequacy? Usually it's a combination of stress and fear. Well, the data is trickling in (here's a postcard now) and it all points in the same direction. Exercise is one of the best ways to alleviate stress and improve self-image. As you feel better about yourself, fears fall away and symptoms of sexual inadequacy often disappear.

As Jack LaLanne says: "Show me a man who's out of condition and I'll show you a man who very often just can't make it sexually. Because sex can never be fully satisfying to a man or his mate if he is run down, tired and weak, or if he is so tense that he can't concentrate on the greatest of pleasures. Besides, his uncomely physique can hardly excite a woman or give him the pride and assurance he needs to make the experience a truly exciting one for both of them."

You tell 'em, Jack baby.

HOW SEX WORKS

To understand how stress can affect sex, you need to understand how sex works. This is important. Listen up.

In the early stages of sexual arousal, the body's parasympathetic system takes command by relaxing the artery walls in the pelvic area, allowing them to dilate. Once done, the blood flows in faster than it flows out. In women, that causes vaginal lubrication as well as swelling of the vulva, clitoris, and vaginal walls. In men, it causes an erection.

As things get hot, the body's sympathetic system takes hold. This causes the pulse rate to quicken, breathing to speed up, and muscles to tense. This tensing of muscles leads to that "oh-my-god" feeling a woman gets just before the muscular contractions of an orgasm, or that a man gets before ejaculation.

But here's where stress comes in. If your mind and body are tied up somewhere else, you can't relax during sex and the whole delicate balance often gets thrown off, causing the sympathetic system to jump the gun. Dealing with stress isn't easy. What has become clear though is that the old ways just don't work. Having a glass of wine or firing up a joint might relax the mind, but it plays tricks on the body, interfering with the spinal reflexes needed for sexual response. Putting alcohol or drugs in your system before sex is like putting low octane gas in your car. It affects performance by really screwing up the timing.

The answer, many psychologists are starting to realize, is exercise. Simply: the more you get your system into sync, the easier you'll be able to deal with stress, and the more pleasurable sex can become.

SOME SCIENTIFIC STUFF

You want proof that exercise helps your sex life, we found proof. First, there's a 1982 Ohio University study that explored the relationship between physical exercise and sexual behavior. It tested "average" students against those who spent more time in the gym. The results? Both frequency of sexual behavior and frequency of sexual activity increased significantly with the amount of physical exercise. In other words, people who exercise regularly are, as a group, just plain hornier.

Another study, also done in 1982, at the Crozier-Chester Medical Center in Chester, Pennsylvania, tried to determine the effects of physical exercise on the process of fantasizing. Forty college students were shown inkblot cards under two sets of circumstances. First, while just sitting in a lounge. And then, while pedaling a stationary bicycle at mild levels of exertion. Libidinal responses were seen as much more striking while the subjects were engaged in physical activity. In plain English, exercise—even something as simple as riding a bike—caused these people to fantasize more and become, as they say in the scientific journals, just plain hornier.

BACK TO REAL LIFE

We weren't yet aware of the scientific findings when we came upon Candi Coleman in a Los Angeles health club.

"Why do I work out?" Candi said, "Because I get off on it." At first, we didn't know what to make of her. She'd get on the stationary bike and ride hard for a while, breathing heavily. Then she would stand up in the stirrups and do sprints. Well, once she got going, her whole body started to change. The look on her face went from exertion to pure pleasure. Toward the end of each sprint, she would begin to moan loudly before sitting down again, letting her inner thighs caress the seat.

All heads on the training floor would turn to watch Candi, who was now in a world of her own. The sounds she made while working out were clearly the same sounds most people make during sex. With each sprint, Candi would moan louder and longer until finally, on her last sprint, she would let out a huge scream, the kind that would make Bob Beamon jump.

"I almost always have an orgasm on the bike," Candi says. "I've learned to work it just right now. I get up enough speed to get my blood flowing, and soon I can feel myself starting to swell down there. Each time I come down and touch the bike seat, I feel more of a tingle. Then

I rev my body up again and the tingle gets stronger. I have almost complete control over it now. I can keep the routine going for a full fifteen minutes before I come."

Candi, a production assistant with a major movie studio, is now talking about getting into competitive bike racing. She might never cross the finish line first, but she'll sure have the most fun getting there.

You talk to trainers and you hear a lot of sex stories. They try to help them along as much as they can. There was a client in a New York gym who used to achieve orgasm on the Nautilus leg curl machine because the exercise causes you to press your pelvis against the body pad. The trainers would keep her on this machine forever.

But sexually stimulating exercises aren't limited to women clients. At another New York gym, some female trainers got a pretty stiff warning from management for putting all their male clients on the Versa-Climber just so they could watch their buns move up and down. The numbers they yelled to each other across the floor had nothing to do with the amount of reps. It was purely a beefcake scoring system.

And where does all this bring us? To a pretty clear knowledge that sex and exercise work together very well indeed. We hope you've heard enough to follow Bob Beamon's example and not worry about one affecting the other. You can do both and do both well. Casey Stengel probably put it best when referring to his World Championship New York Yankees: "It isn't sex that wrecks these guys," he said, "it's staying up all night looking for it."

HURTS
SO
GOOD

This all started a few years ago. It was about 490 B.C. The Greeks, having just won a battle over invading Persians at a place called Marathon, wanted to spread the good news. With the phone lines down, they sent out a soldier and champion runner named Phidippides to carry the cry of victory to the folks back home in Athens, this being an away game. Phidippides set out as fast as his feet would take him and ran the full twenty-five miles from the battlefield to the capital. When he got to the center of town, he shouted, "Rejoice, we conquer." And then he dropped dead, a victim of the world's first recorded sports-related injury.

While there are those who would argue that Achilles had preceded him (he had a bum knee or something), it is a clear fact that sports injuries go back as far as sport itself. Through the years, the injuries have changed with the sports. Gout had its heyday. In more recent years, tennis elbow, runner's knee, and shoulder tendinitis have shared the spotlight. Now that everyone's in the gym, it's not enough to know the right exercise. You need to know the status injuries. Rotator cuff tears and bursitis from heavy pumping are good. A torn gluteus from serious squatting is a nice touch. Arthroscopic surgery is very in. But bad backs are out. People who work at Sears have bad backs. Never admit to this unless you've thrown your back out while weight lifting. That's okay. But only fools shovel snow. And they buy their shovels at Sears.

Trust us. If you work out hard, sooner or later you're going to get injured. We'll give you some advice in this chapter about how to avoid injury, but we're only going through the motions there. Face it: whether it's a simple pull or a torturous tear, you're going to get hurt. It just goes with the territory. And when it happens, you should know how to make the best of it.

Take your basic ski bum—the guy who sits around the lodge with his leg in a cast propped up on a chair and surrounded by beautiful women. "Ah yes," he says, as they hang on his every word, "I'm afraid it's a compound fracture. You see, I was going for the course record on the giant slalom and I just cut that last gate a little too tight." His audience is impressed and sympathetic. They would be neither if he told them the truth—that he slipped on the ice trying to get his bags out of the Volkswagen.

There are other ways to use injury as a psychological ploy. One is something we call preemptive injury. Other people call it covering your ass. Let's say you and some friends are sitting outside a classroom waiting to enter an aerobics session. You notice an attractive member of the opposite sex nearby. You want to impress. Fine. First reach down and massage your shin. Then explain in a clear voice that you've been suffering fron shin splints and that you really hope you'll be able to finish the class without too much pain. It's a can't-lose situation. If you make it, you'll be admired for your strength, courage, and determination. If you fail, you'll get the sympathy vote. Poor baby, tell me where it hurts.

Any good athlete wears his injuries as a sign of valor and honor. The Ace bandage is the Purple Heart of the eighties, to be worn unashamedly for all to admire. But, like the Purple Heart, the injury must occur on the field of battle. In this case, the gym. And it must be the right sort of injury. Only Frank Burns got a Purple Heart for cutting himself shaving. You'll want to find something more adventurous. To aid you in choosing a satisfactory injury, we offer you the Insider's Injury Status Guide, complete with status value ratings from 1 to 10. Let's go head to toe:

UPPER BODY INJURIES

Shoulder tendinitis: Generally located deep inside the deltoid at the most lateral aspect of the shoulder. (Don't you just love these technical terms? They go better than wrapped weenies at cocktail parties.) Shoulder tendinitis can be caused by bench pressing too heavily or by doing too many dips or pushups. It's long lasting and one of the heavy hitter injuries. Treat it with ice after every workout. Use it as an excuse from doing heavy weights or working out too long. *Status value:* 9.

Bursitis: You have these little sacs of fluid in your shoulder called bursa. There are several of them, the most important of which is the subacromial, located at the front of the shoulder. When one of these bursea becomes inflamed, from a weight pressing exercise or from severe overuse, you end up with bursitis. And while bursitis is a nice valid injury that is often chronic, and a good hedge against too much work, it sounds like something that only old people get. Cranky old people. *Status value:* 5.

Rotator cuff tears: An injury to any of the four deep muscles (if you're a name dropper: supraspinatus, infraspinatus, subcapularis, and the ever-popular teres minor) that support the shoulder in its capsule. Rotator cuff (usually called "rotator cup" by Joe Garagiola) was very popular among sports figures several years ago, especially with washed-up relief pitchers. A major cause is overhead lifting. While this one has a nice, athletic sound to it, it is a bit passé. Perhaps you could tell people you once pitched for the Yankees. Who didn't? *Status value:* 7.

Elbow tendinitis: Your basic tennis elbow. It's caused by a forced hyperextension or by a radical twisting of the forearm. In the gym, you can get it by going up and down too fast doing chin-ups or by locking out your elbows doing dips. While this injury does have the fine characteristic of being caused by long abuse, it is still considered terribly sport specific. *Status value:* 6.

Back spasms: Don't admit to this being a chronic condition. And never refer to it simply as a "bad back." This one treads a very thin line between jockdom and wimpiness. If you tell people you got it from doing a heavy deadlift or by slipping while doing some intricate maneuver during an aerobic dance class, you'll get by. Make sure you talk about how many times you've done the same thing without any ill effect. This will give you a chance to expound on your dedication to regular exercise and let you make the best of a mediocre injury. *Status value:* 4.

LOWER TORSO INJURIES

Hernia: Try to talk about abuse from heavy weight lifting. Better yet, don't mention it at all. Just watch where you cough. *Status value:* 1.

Groin pull: A nice conversational injury. But never point. It's usually indicated by a sharp pain aggravated by stretching. It'll only keep you on the inactive list for a few days. It happens while running, twisting, or jumping. If you want to be real macho about it, tell them you did it while squatting. No one will make fun of a heavy squatter. *Status value:* 6.

LEG INJURIES

Chondromalacia patellae: This one's a beaut. It rolls off the tongue, sounds very impressive, but it's not debilitating. It's a general wearing away of the cartilage behind the knee and a softening of the kneecap (patella) itself. Pain and swelling are generally accompanied by a crunching in the knee. Sounds worse than it is. Often "runner's knee" is diagnosed as chondromalacia, but they are quite distinct. Chondromalacia generally implies a long history of exercise, especially running. Be sure not to shrug it off, though. As with all knee injuries, see a doctor. Usually, he'll tell you to ice it after activity, wear a brace and try to work on the support muscles around the knee. Once this baby's in check though, play it for all it's worth. Talk about it freely. You'll achieve elite status if you handle it right. *Status value:* 10.

Runner's knee: Usually caused by excessive pronation of the foot while running. The kneecap ends up rubbing against the femur—which means the knee bone's connected to the shin bone a little too tightly. It can be caused by flat feet, running on a banked surface (such as a city street), or by wearing the wrong shoes. Usual treatment will have you inserting an orthodic into your shoe to prevent the pronation or rolling. There is very little glamour in this. It should only be referred to as a temporary condition (while you're waiting for the orthodic insert to be made). In fact, the orthodics have much greater status value than the injury itself. Runner's knee, by the way, affects more than runners. You can pick it up in an aerobics class or from playing pickup basketball. *Status value:* 3; with orthodics: 5.

Torn medial meniscus: The medial meniscus is sort of a shock absorber for your knee. Technically, it's a fibrocartilage that deepens the knee socket. It can be torn either by a direct blow or by twisting. You'll find this injury a lot now in aerobic dancers. In its earlier incarnation, it was the curse of runners who stepped in too many potholes. This one has a nice medical sound to it, but unlike chondromalacia, it's a very major injury and is most often treated by surgery. It just won't heal itself. That's the bad news. The good news is that the most common form of surgery for meniscal tears or ruptures is arthroscopy, a procedure that's an out-and-out 10 in status value. Having your knee "scoped" will automatically catapult you to jock stardom. "Scoping" the knee involves the insertion of a tube that, with the help of fiberoptics, allows a surgeon to find and remove the damaged tissue, such as a floating bit of cartilage or, in this case, a torn meniscus. The procedure has a reputation of allowing you to walk into and out of the hospital. In 1984, when Joan Benoit qualified for the first women's Olympic marathon, she had undergone arthroscopic surgery just three weeks before. If your doctor recommends major surgery over arthroscopy, get another opinion. Better yet, get another doctor. *Status value:* 8; with arthroscopy: 10.

Shin splints: A good old standby. Most often it's caused by having calf muscles that are too tight and shin muscles that are too weak. Almost everyone in your aerobics class will get these at one time or another. The treatment is simple: you stretch the calf muscles and strengthen the shin muscles. You can do this easily by pulling your foot up against an immovable object or against your other foot. This will apply the needed downward pressure. *Status value:* 4.

Sprained ankle: Never call a sprained ankle a sprained

ankle. Instead, describe it as ruptured or partially ruptured ligaments in your ankle. You can't just "walk off" an ankle sprain. Ice, compression, elevation, and lots of rest will help it heal. *Status value* 3; for ruptured ligaments: 6.

Stress fracture: These are small fractures of the foot bones caused by repeated pounding. They're very painful, though not particularly dangerous. The only treatment is ice (to relieve pain and inflammation) and total rest. Make the best out of it. This injury does have a nice ring to it. *Status value:* 7.

EVERYTHING ELSE

Strains, sprains, pulled muscles, torn muscles, broken bones: In sports medicine talk, these are traumatic injuries. That means they didn't deteriorate over a long period of time. More like: boom, you popped one. The status value of any of these is gained from the context in which they occur. Never admit to injuries of sheer clumsiness. If you trip over the briefcase you left at the top of the stairs and sprain your ankle, and while falling, you grab onto the railing, tearing your bicep just before you hit bottom, breaking your collarbone, you can cover it. Just tell them the ankle was a running injury which brought you indoors and forced you to stick to lifting, where you tore your bicep while doing your fourth set of negative chins and broke the collarbone while doing a heavy bench press and letting the weight down too hard. Some folks just might buy it. And that just might make you feel better. You'll find that, while your injuries might give you some pain, the truth hurts much worse.

THE PART WE WARNED YOU ABOUT

And now, not that we think you'll listen to us, a few words on how to avoid injuries.

Don't overtrain. There's a great tendency to do this when starting out. Instant results sound promising. But you'll pay for them. Your body is not a machine. Watch for its warning signals. Pain is a big one.

Bad training methods. Treat your body with as much common sense as you would your car. If you run your car constantly without letting it rest, it's going to overheat. Your body will do worse than that. Be very slow and cautious in increasing your workload and intensity. And try to stick to the methods your body is used to. If you change at all, do it gradually. Don't try to run like a Porsche if God gave you a Fuego.

Know your imperfections. Quite literally, no one's perfect. Whether it's knock-knees or flat feet or an extra curve in the back, we all have our minor problems. If we recognize them and work around them, they might not become major.

Don't start cold. A common cause of injury is lack of flexibility. When your muscles aren't warm, they won't go where you want them to. Take the time to stretch out before you work out. Don't think that just because you've been working out for years, you don't have to warm up anymore. In fact, you have to warm up *even* more. The muscles you've made hard by all your exercise are much more susceptible to injury. That's why Mike Schmidt always pulls his hamstring.

HOW TO TREAT INJURIES

For anything that seems serious (that means anything that hurts for more than a minute), see a doctor. If you can, see an orthopedist. Better yet, see an orthopedist who specializes in sports medicine. In the meantime, follow these simple steps:

Rest. Don't try to work around an injury until you find out what it's all about. When you feel the pain, stop. Don't start again until your doctor tells you to.

Elevation. This is a matter of gravity. If you can, keep the injured area resting higher than your heart. This will help drain excess fluid, as well as keep you rested.

Compression. Wrap an elastic bandage over an ice pack and around the injured area. Don't wrap it too tight. The idea is to limit swelling, not shut off the blood supply. Too much swelling will slow the healing process.

Ice. Yes, once and for all, put ice on any injured area. And not just for the first twenty minutes. As long as it hurts, keep the ice coming. Ice causes the blood vessels to contract, and that decreases internal bleeding caused by the trauma of injury. You want to do this. Blood around a wound only slows healing. When should you use heat directly after an injury? *Never.* By bringing additional blood to the area, heat will not only increase swelling, it will reduce mobility and probably even cause more pain. And those are the hard, cold facts.

SWEATING WITH THE STARS

Celebrities are just like the rest of us, only more so. Take *Playboy* Playmate Cathy St. George. Nah, Hef wouldn't like that. Take **Ed Bradley** from *60 Minutes*. Ed's not much different from you. He puts his Lycra tights on one leg at a time. Here, we'll let him tell you:

"What motivates me to work out?" he says. "I think ego is part of it. I went on vacation a while back weighing 232 pounds. I knew I had to do something about it. The answer was a combination of diet and training. I pretty quickly worked myself down to 195. Why? I like the way I look at 195 a hell of a lot better than I did at 232. I like the way my clothing looks and fits, I like my personal appearance and, on top of that, I just feel better. Carrying that extra weight just drags me down."

Bradley does admit to falling off the weight wagon every so often. "I have periodic binges," he says. "I like to eat ice cream. I like some wine with my meal. So I have to watch myself. I have to make sure I keep working out no matter what. So when that alarm goes off in the morning, I drag myself out of bed and to the gym, no matter what I did the night before. I won't allow myself not to go. And I feel much better for it."

Bradley's been working out seriously for about five years now. His New York gym isn't far away from his apartment. When he's in town, he tries to go there six days a week. He'll do an hour of aerobics every day and then work out with a trainer on Nautilus machines. His favorite exercise? "I hate 'em all," he says.

He is starting to get into the fashion part of it, though. A confirmed T-shirt-and-gym-shorts man, some friends bought him a pair of Lycra tights for Christmas. "It took me a few months to put them on," he says, "but when I finally did, I said, 'Gee, that looks pretty good.' I went out and bought two more pair. Who knows, I might even get myself a pair of high-top Reeboks one day."

Now we can talk about **Cathy St. George.** Hef will never read this far. Just as you thought (you *do* think about this all the time, don't you?) a Playmate's body is a large part of her fortune. To keep her fortune in shape, St. George starts by walking at least fifty blocks a day. Then she does a slow stretch class three days a week. She does very slow aerobic moves, allowing her to work on each part of her body longer. She does some free weights, but not much.

"I'm small," she says. "If I did a lot of weights, I'd build up bulk. I'm pretty short already (her centerfold was actually lifesize). I don't want to feel even shorter. So I work for tone instead of bulk. That makes me feel taller and skinnier.

"That's one of the great things about working out. It does change the way you feel about yourself. It's great for sex. There's just something about all that moving and pumping that makes me feel sexier and more alluring. And when I feel that way, nothing stops me."

We caught up with Palm Beach socialite and avid trumpet lover **Roxanne Pulitzer** while she was on a nonstop *Playboy* tour promoting a provocative pictorial. Pulitzer now works as an aerobics instructor. Her routine is largely a takeoff on Jane Fonda's. She does incorporate some free weights, though. "Everybody's using Heavy Hands now," she says.

Pulitzer is a big believer in workout frequency. "You have to do it at least three times a week just to get your heart rate going," she says. "These people who work out a couple times a week and expect their bodies to change give me a good laugh. Even three times a week will only maintain what you already have going. If you really want to see some improvement, you have to do it at least four times a week. If not, don't even bother. You're only kidding yourself."

For **Daniel J. Travanti,** star of *Hill Street Blues,* working out was no laughing matter. He points to a stationary bike on the second floor of his Santa Monica home. "The bike helped save my life," he says. "During the idle days of my career, I'd just get on the bike and ride and dream. That's when I started taking care of myself. I had coasted for a long time. I'd smoke and drunk way too much. I was on the way out. In big trouble. Then I started channeling my energy, stopped feeling sorry for myself and started going to the gym. And look at me now."

Travanti is a sight all right—six feet one inch, 190 pounds, almost all of it muscle. He works hard at it, but he's not a fanatic. "I'm vain," he says, "but I don't kill myself. I see some guys on their programs and they're so determined to get all of it in every day. I don't need that. I already have enough tension. Exercise is my way of unwinding. It should be fun, not work."

Bill Madlock, the four-time National League batting champion, has a hard time distinguishing between work and fun. If he's not in shape, his work isn't any fun. In the off-season, he goes to a club and works out with a trainer "religiously" at least three times a week.

"I'm really dedicated to it," he says, "but it takes a lot of work. The better you are, the harder it is to stay there. And I couldn't do it without a trainer. I need someone to push me a bit, to ease me through it. It might sound odd for a professional athlete to say that, but, just like with baseball, you do whatever works best for you."

A personal trainer also works best for super race driver **Danny Sullivan.** In winning the 1985 Indy 500, Sullivan had an extra member on his crew. He flew in star trainer Dan Isaacson from L.A. to work with him in the days leading up to the race. "I have to be careful about doing too much with weights," Sullivan says. "I've been wearing a size forty jacket for years, but I went to buy one the other day and I took a forty-two. I just bulk up too quickly. So I try to work more on stamina. When I'm in L.A., I go every day. We'll do chest, back, and triceps one day and the next day do legs and shoulders. You have to rotate the concentration. You just can't go in every day and work on the same areas. You'd kill yourself."

Sullivan, who had bad knees from all the skiing he's done, tries to stay away from running. He does most of his aerobic work on a bike. "I just got a LifeCycle for my house," he says. "They're great. A friend of mine mounted a TV on his, plugged a VCR into it, and pedals for hours at a time watching his favorite movies."

Chris Meade is one of the most important trainers in the country, if client lists are any indication. Meade, who used to work out of New York's Sports Training Institute, is a premier celebrity trainer. Although he prefers to think of his clients more as artists.

"There's a difference between a celebrity and an artist," he says. "There are the **Bianca Jaggers,** who are simply celebrities. She was incredibly demanding. My life had to revolve around her schedule. I worked with her for two years, although it seemed like ten. And then there are artists. Of course, we've made celebrities out of some artists. We've made celebrities from people who get off their asses and do something about a situation. Like **Jane Fonda.** She first came to me when she was doing *Rollover* with Kris Kristofferson. She really got involved with working out. And I give her a lot of credit. A lot of celebrities could have written a book. But she got off her ass and did it."

How does Meade train Fonda? "When Jane comes in," he says, "it's not just her body I'm working on. It's knowing her brain, talking about her last movie with her, her current life situation. What I try to do is make the training time a time for herself, a time she can indulge herself. I tell her: 'Leave all your problems at the front door and pick up your garbage on the way out.'

"And, even though she has her own fitness followers, when she comes in here, I'm leading the dance. A session for her is a combination of basic stretching, aerobics, and strength training. While her basic routine stays the same each time, I'll add or subtract depending on her mood. If she's tense, if I see her shoulders are up near her earlobes, I'll change the routine and not do any weights that day. Just aerobics. There's no reason to add stress."

Artists, Chris Meade says, do need pampering. "When **Jeremy Irons** comes in at four in the afternoon, and I know he's going straight from the gym to a sold-out theater on Broadway, it's up to me to make sure everything goes smoothly. I know in my head that when Jeremy is doing an overhead press with dumbbells, that my concentration has to be 1000 percent. That's my responsibility. I'm like a dentist. I can't have a bad day. It's that much more important working with artists because they'll give themselves any excuse to not do something positive for themselves. As a former performer, I know them all. So when they do come in, they want to be pampered. They expect it. They want care, sympathy, and a sense of passion. It's up to me to help them switch gears. Jeremy might have come from a big meeting or he just might have been out partying a little too much the night before. He comes here for a tune-up, to try to get his performance pacing down. And that's what training does for him—it helps him get his life in order."

Here are a few mostly friendly words from Chris Meade about some of his other celebrated clients:

"**Karan Allen** is the easiest person I've ever worked with. She's not caught up in the celebrity bit. She's very clearheaded and she enjoys the work. That's why we work so well together. She doesn't bring her problems to the floor. Sometimes this becomes more of an analysis session than physical training.

"**Keven Kline** is incredibly spontaneous. He realizes working out is very repetitious. There are only so many ways you can do a bicep curl. So he accepts it like another acting role. He'll start mimicking Richard Gere in *An Officer and a Gentleman*. Instead of complaining about the pain, he'll do lines to give himself an image. He'll put the pain into those lines, the way any good actor uses emotion. He'll turn working out into an acting job.

"**Laura Branigan** is very sensitive and very unassuming. She still feels funny about being recognized. So she has a tendency to pull her shoulders up and bury her head inside her chest. It's like she wants to crawl into a ball. Her posture's going out the window. Her back's bothering her because she's not supporting it enough. And that's all because of the physical manifestations of her emotional stardom. I work to make her forget all that and relax. If stardom is her burden, exercise is her release.

"**John & Caroline Kennedy** can come to me and relax because they don't have to feel on guard and watch everything they say, afraid they might read it the next day in the *New York Post* or the *National Enquirer*. The intimacy I have with my people is more important than that. It's all a matter of trust. Someone who exposes him- or herself to me, who lets their guard down and maybe some tears out—and for me to see physical changes in their body because of this trust—is much more important to me than the chance to blab about when someone had her period on the double hip and back machine."

Tina Turner, who gets more exercise on stage in one night than most people do in a gym all year, likes to work out outdoors, usually playing tennis. It keeps her in fine shape. "I was thin," she says, "before it was fashionable— way back when it was stylish to have a big fanny."

Pat Benatar, an admitted ice cream junkie, is very much into aerobic dancing. "I've taped an hour and a half of exercises to take on the road," she says, "and already I've lost eight pounds."

Susan Sarandon prefers swimming. But when she can't find a pool, she'll do about twenty minutes of sit-ups. She was lifting weights for a while, but found it hard to maintain. "When you have to fly to Greece for a movie, you can't very well take your gym with you."

Jamie Lee Curtis maintains the body of the eighties with light weight lifting, daily sit-ups, and aerobics classes a couple of times a week. . . . **Cheryl Tiegs,** who once weighed 155 pounds, has added calisthenics and weight work to her regular running and tennis routines. . . . **Christie Brinkley** likes to bike, but doesn't like it stationary. She once rode her ten-speed to a win in a seventy-four-kilometer race in Paris. . . .

Bill Cosby has a friend, former Olympic hurdler Josh Culbreath, who times him as he urges him through sprinting workouts. . . . **Kareem Abdul-Jabbar** has added yoga sessions four or five times a week to his strength and flexibility training. . . . Strength training on Nautilus machines helped **Patrick Ewing** add thirty pounds to his postadolescent seven-foot frame. . . . **Marvelous Marvin Hagler** does 200 sit-ups a day as a fight nears. That's in addition to his fifty conventional pushups and twenty with each arm. . . . **Lyle Alzado** spends three-day spurts in the gym, working two and a half hours the first day solely on his upper body. . . . **Steve Garvey** spends thirty minutes a day just stretching before he moves on to serious weight training. . . .

Paul Newman does 200 sit-ups a day, no matter what. . . . **James Caan** does at least fifty bench dips. . . . **Nick Nolte** does one hundred pushups, one hundred sit-ups, then one hundred jumping jacks. Then he runs two miles. . . . **Chris Evert** has become a yoga fanatic. . . . **Roy Scheider, Roberta Flack, Lee Radziwill** and **Ralph Lauren** are all heavily into "adult gymnastics"—tumbling, headstands, and such. . . . And **Sylvester Stallone** goes through a five-hour daily workout designed to burn up about 12,000 calories. Some days it works. But some days, he says, he feels really woozy. Eh, you wanna make somethin' of it?

EXPLODING THE MYTHS

There is gospel and there is garbage. In the fitness game, many self-proclaimed experts are quick to pass off the latter for the former. A fitness expert, of course, is anyone who's been to a gym more than once. And if that person happens to know how to put a pin in a Nautilus machine, we're talking guru. How then do you separate the good advice from the bullshit? We have our own favorite expert on that subject. In the profound words of Marvin Gaye: "Believe half of what you see and none of what you hear."

Here then is a grapevine of talking trash. Monstrous

myths. The whole untruth. Read all of this chapter. And believe half of it.

Working out builds muscle and, since muscle is heavier than fat, working out will make you gain weight. Wrong. Quick, which is heavier: a pound of feathers or a pound of gold? You see, muscle isn't heavier than fat, just denser. That means, when you're fit, you can carry the same amount of weight as you used to and still look thinner. "But," you say, "I'm working out more and eating less and I'm still gaining weight." Poppycock. The only way you gain weight is by taking in more calories than you burn off. It might not be much. That yogurt shake at the juice bar or the quick brewsky after a run. But it's enough. And it's simple math. If you sweat off fifty calories and cool yourself by drinking down a hundred, you're gonna gain weight. Remember, there is no such thing as light beer.

When you stop exercising, all your muscle will turn to fat. Don't worry. Muscle and fat are two different things. It is likely that once you stop exercising for any long period your muscles will start to lose tone and you'll start to lose power and strength. Muscle won't turn to fat though because muscle is fatless. But muscle isn't weightless. You'll want to keep this in mind if you're planning any crash diets. While fat will be the first to go, you'll eventually start to lose muscle, too. This is why exercise is one of the most important parts of a diet. Muscle, to remain muscle, needs to keep generating itself. The only way to do that is to exercise, watch between-meal treats, brush three times a day, keep your shoes shined, and, of course, drink plenty of water.

You shouldn't drink too much water when you exercise.

Just the opposite. Drink as much as you want. Thirst is your body's way of telling you it needs water. So drink when you're thirsty. If you're running on a treadmill and you get thirsty, stop and get a drink and then start again. You won't lose much in the way of momentum and you'll probably be able to run a lot longer. Smart marathoners know all this. No matter how much they drink during a race, they can't replace all the fluid they lose. For anyone doing serious exercise, drinking too much water is just about impossible. On the average, your body sweats out thirty-three ounces of water during a half hour of exercise. In the same period, it can absorb only nine ounces. So drink up. This is deficit spending.

There is no such thing as "spot reducing." That ain't necessarily so. You can reduce the size of one part of your body without reducing your whole body. If you work out your abdominal muscles, your stomach will probably be flatter, but that doesn't mean the size of your legs will change. The idea here is to think of fat and muscle differently. Exercise itself won't make all the fat go away. But the muscles underneath the fat in a given area will become much firmer through exercise, giving that part of your body a trimmer look. This is called cheating.

A *few* minutes of exercise a day will get you in shape. You wish. A few minutes are better than none, but if you want to see any real results, you really need to work at it. For any significant cardiovascular improvement, we're taking at least ten hard minutes a day, bare bones. If you want to get serious, make it at least a half hour three times a week.

You can flatten your stomach in a flash. If you already

bought the books that tell you how to do junk like this (you did, didn't you?), this news flash comes a little too late. The only real way to flatten your stomach is through a combination of diet and exercise. And you can't do that in thirty seconds or thirty days or whatever those people are promising you. Even endless sit-ups won't do it. Again, that will just tighten the stomach muscle under the fat. To get rid of fat, you need to get rid of calories. And sit-ups or pushups won't really do that. Pushaways will. Just count to three and push yourself away from the dinner table before dessert shows up.

If you work out every day, you're overtraining. This is partially true. If you work out with heavy weights every day, you're not only overtraining, you're stupid. But all that means is you shouldn't go all out every time. Don't think of the days in between heavy workouts as days off. Think of them as light days. Use them for stretching and other easy aerobic work. It'll make you breathe easier and you won't feel like a stiff.

Working out with ankle weights will make you lighter on your feet. Those lead links you strap on might make you *feel* lighter on your feet, but what they really do is give you uneven muscle development. They strengthen your quadriceps without strengthening your hamstrings. That's enough to rip you up. Also, if you run for a long time with ankle wieghts, you won't develop speed, just shin splints.

Getting "psyched up" makes for a better workout. Psyching, yes, but it's a matter of direction. Prevailing theories these days recommend something that's more like "psyching down." Remember, relaxation and concentration are key for mental preparation in exercise and sport. Many top athletes tell of feelings of sluggishness, even sickness, before their greatest performances. So jumping up and down to get your adrenaline flowing may do your workout more harm than good. Besides, it'll only make your socks fall down.

Protein powders help you lose weight. Protein powders help you gain weight. Look at any health or fitness magazine and you'll see tons of ads for these things. The way they work is simple. They are lower in calories than the meal they replace. So you lose weight. While protein powders do provide the body with essential amino acids (useful in building and repairing muscle), they just don't make good energy food. Complex carbohydrates are much better. And those carbohydrates won't leave you feeling as crappy as most protein powders will.

On the other end of the scale, protein powders that help you gain weight are high in calories and are taken in addition to other meals. They never replace a meal. So you gain weight simply because you're taking in more calories. You don't need a medical degree for that one. The fact that the powders are high in protein, though, does you little good, unless your normal diet is terribly low in protein. Your body isn't dumb. It only uses as much protein as it needs (about 0.8 grams per kilogram of body weight per day or about 11 percent of your normal daily caloric intake). The surplus is disposed of within four hours of consumption. Gone to visit the Tidy Bowl man.

Eating lots of meat and drinking lots of milk will make you healthy. You might want to be very careful about how you break this one to your mother, but your diet should consist mostly of complex carbohydrates (such as fruits, vegetables, grains and starches). Don't get us wrong. We're not saying you should cut out meat and milk completely. Nobody ever died from a great cheeseburger. And your body certainly does need some protein and calcium and iron and other minerals. But probably not as much as you think. And certainly you don't need all the fat associated with milk and meat. And the gas . . . you could just die.

Working out can cure what ails you. Let's start with the common hangover. Many of us do. While there is a chance that working out will speed up your metabolism and help remove the alcohol from your stream, you're probably better just sleeping it off. If you must work out, take it easy. The alcohol in your system makes your muscles less flexible and less effective. So don't go trying the same amount of weight that you normally would. This could hurt you. Instead, stress cardiovascular work. But don't push too hard there either or you'll get sick and your head will fall off. Also, recovery time from a workout with alcohol in your system will be much slower. Lactic acid just doesn't make a great mixer for alcohol.

If you have a cold, an increased metabolic rate may help clear your sinuses for a bit, but in the long run, you'll just run yourself down and open yourself up to potential injury. Stay in bed, drink plenty of fluids, and call your trainer in the morning.

Working out will improve your posture. Working out will strengthen your muscles. Standing up straight will improve your posture. If your posture is poor because your back or stomach is weak, then toning those muscles will help. But only if you make a conscious effort to stand straighter. If your posture is bad because your muscles are too tight, then stretching might help a little, but you're still going to have to stand up straighter. How many times do we have to tell you this?

Stress is bad for you. There are all different kinds of stress. There is pushing-to-make-a-sale stress. There is rushing-to-meet-a-deadline stress. And there is trying-to-get-your-cat-off-the-roof stress. But those are more mental stresses. In order for you to make any real gains in your exercise, you're going to have to put some stress on your system. You'll either have to elevate your heart rate or push more weight than you normally would. The idea here is that by putting a lot of stress on your system for short periods, you'll be better able to handle less stress the rest of the time. This is true in real life as well as in the gym. If you get your cat off the roof safely once, you won't worry about it so much the next time. This really works. Except for Siamese cats. We're not sure why. Maybe it's because they don't stand up straighter.

You can't change your body when you're past thirty. A fifty-one-year-old client at the Sports Training Institute tells this story: "For twenty years, I've been going to the same tailor in Toronto. He has my pattern. When I need new suits, I give him a call and tell him to make up a gray herringbone and a navy pinstripe and he ships them off to me and they fit like a glove. Except last winter. The suits were too tight. I called him up. 'Max,' I said, 'you screwed up.' 'Impossible,' he said, 'you must have gained weight.' I caught the next plane up to Toronto. It turns out both of us were wrong. From working out, my body has changed shape. My chest is bigger and my waist is smaller. I had to have all the pants taken in. That was the good news. Now what am I going to do with all of those tight jackets? Being in shape is going to cost me a fortune."

You haven't achieved a thing unless you can bench press your own body weight. Strength is only partially a function of body size. Your genes play a big part. Genetically, you might be blessed with a greater abundance of "slow twitch" muscle fibers and would be better suited to becoming a marathon runner than a power lifter. Also, when you talk about lifting your own weight, lean muscle mass is really the determining factor. If you're carrying around thirty extra pounds, don't even think about trying to lift your weight unless that thirty pounds is solid muscle. Finally, women aren't built the same as men. Some of you might have noticed that.

A hot shower, a whirlpool, and steam are the best things after a hard workout. If you've just worked out and your body is overheated and you're sweating a whole lot, the last thing you want to do is step into the whirlpool. Perspiration is the body's way of cooling itself. As the perspiration sits on the surface of the skin, it evaporates. This cools the blood underneath the skin. A steam bath, whirlpool, or hot shower puts a great strain on this natural cooling system, preventing it from doing what comes naturally. As it tries harder and harder to work, a great deal of strain is put on your heart. This is not good. Also, if you're dehydrated from a workout, added heat could dehydrate you to very dangerous levels. Always drink water after a workout, and take a cool shower before going into a steam bath, sauna, or whirlpool. And, of course, always take off your socks.

You should always wear a jockstrap when working out. Women can probably get away without one. And so (surprise, surprise) can men. Your testicles already come with a supporter. It's called the scrotum. And the scrotum is supported by the spermatic cord, which goes from the testicles up to the groin, passing through the wall of the belly into the abdomen. Right there, it's surrounded very tightly by tissue. When that tissue is torn, you get a hernia. A supporter, which only holds up the scrotum, does nothing for those tight tissues. Actually, the only thing a supporter really does is make you sweat more. And that gives you jock itch. You remember jock itch.

No pain, no gain. Sure you have to work hard to get results, but you certainly can make gains without pain. Let's say you spend a half hour riding a stationary bike or taking an aerobics class or playing a quick game of racquetball. You probably won't be suffering much. But will you be making gains? Sure you will. People take the "no pain, no gain" theory much too literally. They use it as an excuse to drive themselves beyond reasonable limits and often only stop when they're too sore or too injured to keep going. When you're weight training, you shouldn't try to "max out" every workout. The bulk of them should be submaximal. Your body makes its best gains when it's well rested. Remember, pushing too hard can not only cause injury, it can cause you to sweat too much. And that gives you jock itch.

You can learn everything you need to know about fitness by reading one book. That's dead wrong. And that's why we're writing a sequel.

ABOUT THE AUTHORS

Maury Z. Levy is editor of *Video Review*, the world's largest video magazine. Previously, he was editor of *Playboy Guides,* a series of special lifestyle handbooks on topics from fashion to fitness. Before that, he was editorial director of *Philadelphia Magazine,* where he won a number of national awards for consumer and investigative reporting. He has written for a host of magazines, from *New York* to *Ladies Home Journal.* His sports background is extensive. He once sparred with Muhammad Ali, beat Billie Jean King in a race across a hotel lobby and, near the end of a *Playboy Interview,* Pete Rose once threatened him with a baseball bat. Levy has one wife, three sons, and 297 pairs of athletic shoes.

Jay Shafran, now an advertising copywriter, was, for several years, the most highly-demanded trainer at New York's famous Sports Training Institute. He was featured as one of the country's top private trainers in a *Sportstyle* magazine feature and has appeared as a fitness expert on a number of television shows. Before joining STI, he worked as a manager of the New York Health and Racquet Club. He has also served as a consultant to a number of other training facilities. His client list contained some of the highest-powered people in New York, including such luminaries as Ed Bradley and Maury Z. Levy.